With thanks for the support of:

Experience the joy of worry-free cycling with Tannus Tyres. Their revolutionary puncture-free tyres enhance your cycling experience and improve your overall lifestyle and well-being. By eliminating the inconvenience of flat tyres, Tannus empower you to embrace a more active and fulfilling lifestyle. Say goodbye to the stress and frustration of unexpected punctures, allowing you to enjoy uninterrupted rides and explore new cycling routes confidently. With their durable and reliable design, Tannus Tyres provide a sense of freedom and relaxation, allowing you to immerse yourself in the beauty of the journey entirely. Rediscover the joy of cycling and elevate your well-being with Tannus Tyres. Visit www.tannus.com to explore their range and embark on your cycling adventures with peace of mind and unwavering enthusiasm.

Embark on a remarkable wellness journey with HINNAO® and experience the extraordinary benefits of their high-stability liposomal liquid drops. These cutting-edge supplements are meticulously crafted for rapid absorption, ensuring their potent nutrients reach their full potential within 60–90 seconds. With their superior bioavailability, surpassing traditional liposomes, HINNAO® sets a new nutrient uptake and effectiveness standard. The range has been in development since 2013. Their unwavering dedication to biotechnology and scientifically proven bioavailability has paved the way for enhanced health span and lifespan. Discover the immense potential of these revolutionary products at www.hinnao.com, where you can uncover the secrets to achieving a harmonious and balanced state of mind. Explore how HINNAO® supports not only physical well-being but also aids in alleviating anxiety, providing you with a comprehensive approach to holistic health and a renewed sense of tranquillity.

EEL Association is a beacon of innovation, seamlessly blending entertainment, entrepreneurship, and lifestyle in the United Kingdom. Their diverse portfolio of exhibitions, festivals, networking events, and parties extends beyond geographical boundaries, engaging audiences nationwide. More than just event organisers, EEL Association cultivates a vibrant community that inspires individuals to unleash their full potential. They create enthralling experiences that entertain and contribute to well-being by fostering a sense of belonging and facilitating meaningful connections. Their inclusive and collaborative approach ignites possibility, fostering personal growth and entrepreneurial spirit. Join their dynamic community at www.eelassociation.com and embark on a captivating journey filled with enriching experiences that positively impact your life and aspirations.

"Outstanding! A needed resource for all of us who have experienced the terror of unexpected anxiety. At last there is a solution!" Dr Joe Vitale, author, *Zero Limits* and *The Miracle*

"Belynder Walia created a transformational masterpiece. In her book *Fix Me: How to Manage Anxiety and Take Control of Your Life*, she helps your mental and emotional well-being with her in-depth method and intuitive wisdom. A must book to read and to share with your family and friends." – Dame Marie Diamond Multiple Global Bestselling #1 Author, *Star in the Secret*, Feng Shui master with more than 1 million online students. www. mariediamond.com

"*Fix Me: How to Manage Anxiety and Take Control of Your Life* by Dr Belynder is a transformative voyage that empowers readers to take control of their mental and emotional well-being. Through practical techniques and insightful guidance, this book provides a roadmap to break free from the grips of anxiety. Discover your inner strength and embark on a journey of self-discovery with this empowering guide." – Bianca Miller Cole, Sunday Times Bestselling Author of *The Business Survival Kit* and *Self Made*.

"Belynder shares how to become more intimate with anxiety, patterns, how to identify triggers and, most importantly, provides a toolkit to work through emotions. A road map of empowerment that serves as an important resource in your journey of self-awareness." – Randy Spelling Life Coach | Speaker | Author of *Unlimiting You: Step Out of Your Past and Into Your Purpose*

"This book is packed with insights, resources and tools that will help improve your mental and emotional wellbeing." – Simon Alexander Ong, bestselling author of *Energize*

"As a mental athlete, my journey has been about training and mastering my mind. Living with chronic pain and enduring multiple surgeries has led me to understand the mind's power in a whole new light. Belynder's book, *Fix Me*, was a revelation in this respect. This book emerges as an indispensable tool for managing the constant discomfort and anxiety that accompany chronic ailments and much more. By teaching us to harness the potential of our minds, *Fix Me* opens the door to a transformative journey that can alter our lives significantly. It is an essential read for those seeking a new perspective on managing pain and anxiety and improving their overall condition." – Tansel Ali, 4-Time Australian Memory Champion

"As the Editor-in-Chief of a magazine dedicated to mental health topics, and with a personal passion for this subject matter, I wholeheartedly recommend *Fix Me: How to Manage Anxiety and Take Control of Your Life*. It's a powerful resource that empowers individuals to conquer anxiety and embrace their inner strength. With practical techniques and inspiring insights, this book serves as a guiding light on the path to personal growth and healing." – Caroline Winkvist, Editor-in-Chief, *Brainz Magazine*

"*Fix Me* is more than just a book – it is a trusted companion on your journey to overcome anxiety and embrace personal growth. With its wealth of knowledge, practical exercises, and compassionate guidance, you will reclaim control over your mental and emotional well-being. Delve into the depths of self-understanding and adopt powerful coping strategies, as you embark on a transformative path towards a life defined by peace, resilience, and fulfilment. Embrace the power within you, break free from the grip of anxiety, and discover the joy of living your best life after reading *Fix Me...*" – Dr Bal Pawa MD, Integrative Physician | TedX Speaker, Co-Founder Westcoast Women's Clinic, and author of *The Mind-Body Cure*

"A special thanks to Dr Belynder for this book, the topics around anxiety, fear and self confidence running a business organisation are so relevant to what we do daily, monthly and throughout the year for us to keep fulfilling our mission and vision of EEL. Some of the tools and techniques mentioned to overcome your inhibitions and uncertainties within your mindset whether you are in business or daily life is a must read and take away you will have. There are many such motivational books and authors, however, the simplicity of connecting with you is what Dr Belynder shares with her readers and knowing her for all these years it will resonate with you after *Fix Me*. A truly beautiful read for all ages and audiences who sometimes need that 1-extra hope to succeed and *Fix me* will certainly levitate your spirits." – Mr Joydeep Das, Chairperson and Founder, EEL Association: www.eelassociation.com

"*Fix Me*: your trusted companion in overcoming anxiety, offering knowledge, exercises, and guidance. Belynder knows how to help you reclaim control, embrace self-understanding, and adopt coping strategies for a life of peace, resilience, and fulfilment. I was very impressed by this book; it helps you discover joy and live your best life." – Youngki Lee, CEO and founder, Tannus Tires: www.tannus.com

"*Fix Me* delivers a wholehearted approach to conquering anxiety and the impact of it on our mind, body, and well-being. Not only does it acknowledge the challenges, but allows one to connect to Belynder via self reflection; a raw and authentic presence. With the provision of hope and practical tools to empower healing and growth, *Fix Me* allows for a safe space to accept, flourish from and overcome anxiety. As a clinician and intuitive empath passionate in raising awareness of mental health, I see a guiding light to self-transformation and see *Fix Me* as core to anyone's recovery." – Dr Jigna Patel Lead Clinical Advisor – Hinnao Technology GP, Aesthetic Clinician and Founder of Vedaskin

"Whilst societal and technological progress has undoubtedly brought many benefits in terms of keeping in touch with one's friends and family around the globe, that same progress can easily create an environment where stress and anxiety get amplified to detrimental levels. Pressure to be always available and always responsive in the online world can sometimes get out of hand. *Fix Me*, provides a practical and insightful guide for anyone who may need help to navigate the complexities of modern life. Especially for young individuals finding their path in life and still working on defining their own personas, this book will help readers to manage their emotions and mental health in a more holistic way and provide a path to get the most out of their precious lives." – Raj Gawera VP and Managing Director, Samsung Cambridge and Samsung Denmark.

"As someone who has experienced firsthand the extraordinary power of a focused mindset when facing life-altering circumstances, I found Belynder Walia's *Fix Me* relevant, compelling, and remarkably instructive. Her writing is painfully honest, and her desire to help others shines through." – Scott Burrows, Speaker, and Author of *Vision Mindset Grit*

"Dr Belynder Walia's *Fix Me: How to Manage Anxiety and Take Control of Your Life* is a compassionate and empowering guide that offers practical tools and valuable insights for anyone seeking to navigate mental health challenges and anxiety. Through relatable storytelling and evidence-based practices, this book sheds light on the path to healing and self-empowerment. A must-read resource for those on a journey towards improved mental well-being." – Rhonda Swan. Founder of Women Gone Wild book series, CEO of Unstoppable Branding Agency

"I have met Belynder on several occasions and she is one of the most inspirational people I have come across in over 30 years in business. I would recommend all my clients to read her latest book *Fix Me* or anybody else who is in need of any help with their anxiety which I know plagues so many people. She is one of the top people in this field and I am sure it is going to alter many people's lives for the good. She is on the side of the Angels!" – Keith Bishop, Owner and Founder of Keith Bishop Associates, www.kba.agency

FIX ME

How to Manage Anxiety and
Take Control of Your Life

Belynder Walia

WILEY

Registered office
John Wiley & Sons, Inc., 111 River Street, Hoboken, NJ 07030, USA

John Wiley & Sons Ltd, The Atrium, Southern Gate, Chichester, West Sussex, PO19 8SQ, United Kingdom

Editorial Office
John Wiley & Sons Ltd, The Atrium, Southern Gate, Chichester, West Sussex, PO19 8SQ, United Kingdom

For details of our global editorial offices, customer services, and more information about Wiley products visit us at www.wiley.com.

Wiley also publishes its books in a variety of electronic formats and by print-on-demand. Some content that appears in standard print versions of this book may not be available in other formats.

Designations used by companies to distinguish their products are often claimed as trademarks. All brand names and product names used in this book are trade names, service marks, trademarks or registered trademarks of their respective owners. The publisher is not associated with any product or vendor mentioned in this book.

Library of Congress Cataloging-in-Publication Data

Names: Walia, Belynder, author.
Title: Fix me : safely become your own therapist & manage anxiety / Dr. Belynder Walia.
Description: Hoboken, NJ : Wiley-Capstone, 2024. | Includes index.
Identifiers: LCCN 2023035603 (print) | LCCN 2023035604 (ebook) | ISBN 9780857089694 (paperback) | ISBN 9780857089717 (adobe pdf) | ISBN 9780857089700 (epub)
Subjects: LCSH: Anxiety. | Well-being.
Classification: LCC BF575.A6 W33 2024 (print) | LCC BF575.A6 (ebook) | DDC 152.4/6—dc23/eng/20230816
LC record available at https://lccn.loc.gov/2023035603
LC ebook record available at https://lccn.loc.gov/2023035604

Cover Design: Wiley
Cover Image: Safety Pins © K3Star / Adobe Stock;
Torn Paper © Yeti Studio / Adobe Stock
Author Photo by Avni Walia

SKY10055554_091823

Contents

CONTENTS

Preface

Anxiety is a formidable adversary that can leave the strongest among us utterly helpless. As someone who has experienced firsthand the debilitating effects of anxiety, I know all too well how it can take a toll on your mental and emotional well-being. My journey of self-discovery and healing began during a very trying time of my life.

For an excruciating eight years, I endured the emotional turmoil of in vitro fertilisation (IVF) treatment, the unspoken grief of multiple invasive procedures, the heart-wrenching pain of three miscarriages, and a life-threatening surgery that loomed over me like a dark cloud. Losing my twins was an indescribable pain that made me feel like I would never recover. The financial burden of IVF treatment added to my anxiety, and when it all got to be too much for my husband, he left me—feeling alone and overwhelmed with grief. To make matters worse, I lost my job and home, plunging me into debt. It was truly a dark time in my life, but it taught me invaluable lessons about the importance of seeking help and the power of resilience.

Fortunately, I had a great network of family and friends to support me during those dark days. My mother's wise words and guidance gave me clarity and hope when I felt lost. My brother Jazz and his wife Jinny, along with their three amazing children—Avni, Jivan, and Jia—brought joy and laughter into my life, reminding me of the good in the world. And my cousins, Ravinder, Rani, and Rupee, were a constant source of comfort and support, lending an ear whenever

I needed it. I couldn't have made it through without them. Oh, and let's not forget my heart, soul, and beautiful best friend, my Newfoundland dog, Chico—his unwavering love and presence were a daily reminder that I was never alone.

Amidst the turmoil of battling the internal villain (anxiety), I discovered that the true path to healing comes from within. The power of self-love, self-healing, and self-relationship therapy opened my eyes to the knowledge that we have a superhero within us all. This personal journey inspired me to put pen to paper and start writing. Beginning with journalling and then venturing into magazines and fictional stories, writing became my ultimate form of healing. It wasn't long before I founded Serene Lifestyles, an online and on-set psychotherapy service, where I worked with people from across the globe and from all walks of life, including celebrities, public figures, and even royalty. I discovered that no matter how successful people may appear, everyone has moments of brokenness, and the only way to move forward on an inner healing journey is to find a way to make the first move and just start.

That's why I'm excited to share this comprehensive self-care guide with you. In the following pages, I will delve into the strategies, techniques, and insights I have gained through my own healing journey and professional experience. This guide is intended to be a companion, a source of support, and a roadmap to help you navigate your own path towards self-care, healing, and resilience.

Remember, you are not alone in your struggles. Within the pages of this book, I hope you will find solace, inspiration, and practical guidance to empower you on your own personal journey. It's time to embrace the superhero within and embark on a transformative and fulfilling path towards well-being.

Wishing you serenity and strength.

Acknowledgements

I want to express my heartfelt gratitude to the following individuals who have played an instrumental role in shaping my life and this book. Their unwavering support, love, and guidance have been invaluable throughout my journey.

First and foremost, I want to thank my family. My mother Ravinder Walia, for being an incredible role model and showing me what it means to be resilient, fearless, and full of love and gratitude. Your strength and unwavering belief in me have been a constant source of inspiration. My brother Jazz Walia and his beautiful wife Jinny Walia, thank you for always being there for me, providing unwavering support and a shoulder to lean on. Your love and encouragement have given me the courage to face any challenge that comes my way. Also, thanks to my amazing sister Jatinder Paul and her husband Manoj Paul, and my brother Paul Walia and his lovely wife Neelam Walia. I have so much love for you all.

I am deeply grateful to Ravinder Goomer, Rani Goomer, and Rupee Chagar, my cousins, for being incredible and offering constant support and belief in me. Your presence and willingness to lend an ear have meant the world to me. I thank Abhinav Saksena for believing in me and my work. From you all, your confidence in my abilities has been a driving force behind this endeavour.

To Linzi Day, my wonderful mentor and an incredible author, without you this book would not have been possible. Thank you for your faith in my abilities and firm guidance throughout this process. Your insights and expertise have been invaluable, and I am forever grateful for your assistance.

I also want to acknowledge my nieces and nephews, Jasmin Walia, Danny Walia, Madhvi Devi Paul, Amrit Kishan Paul, Avni Walia, Jivan Walia, Arjun Sudev Paul, and Jia Walia. Your presence in my life has taught me the true meaning of motherhood and the importance of cherishing every precious moment.

A special mention goes to those who are no longer with me. My generous, loving father, Harcharan Singh Walia, whom I sadly only knew briefly and my loyal and beloved Newfoundland dog and faithful companion, Chico, whose unconditional love and unwavering presence gave me solace and comfort during even the darkest times.

I would also like to thank Gus Miklos, my dedicated developmental editor, for his hard work and commitment to ensuring the quality and clarity of this book. I am grateful to Annie Knight, my commissioning editor, for her belief in my work and continuous support throughout the writing process. And to the Wiley team, your encouragement and enthusiasm have been truly uplifting.

Lastly, I appreciate all those who have contributed to this book in various ways, whether through their feedback, encouragement, or expertise. Your contributions have been integral to shaping this book, and I am deeply thankful for your involvement. A special thanks to each and every person who has touched my life and contributed to this book, thank you from the bottom of my heart. Your love, support, and belief in me have made this journey possible.

About The Author

....

"Born in London, United Kingdom, Belynder Walia embarks on a journey as a catalyst for personal growth and empowerment rooted in her Indian British heritage. Her path, woven from the fusion of cultures, is a testament to her unwavering commitment to positive change and adaptability. Anchored in a deep dedication to psychology, mindfulness, and holistic well-being, Belynder has honed a diverse identity as a skilled psychotherapist, anxiety expert, celebrated author, speaker, and fervent advocate for nurturing inner harmony.

Belynder's voice radiates as an authentic guiding light in mental health. With a distinct emphasis on nurturing a profound self-relationship, she adeptly leads individuals on an introspective journey. Her insights unveil the transformative potential of comprehending emotions, triggers, and responses, particularly when facing anxiety. Through her artful storytelling and vulnerability sharing of personal experiences, Belynder lays out a pathway that inspires a compassionate, encouraging, and relatable inner dialogue, promoting resilience and developing an elevated sense of well-being. Her message transcends the mere act of overcoming challenges; it encapsulates acknowledging genuine self and navigating life's intricate individuality with renewed self-awareness, acceptance, and love."

Introduction

Have you ever experienced the overwhelming grip of dread, as if the world is conspiring against you? Do you find yourself trapped in a sea of worry and despair, struggling to find a way to break free? Anxiety can be an unyielding force, leaving you feeling helpless and isolated. It may manifest as physical symptoms like headaches, stomach aches, and heart palpitations, seemingly without a clear cause. You might witness others living your desired life while you feel like yours is slipping away. These experiences are all too familiar, leaving you longing for guidance and support. But fear not, for the paths to transform these thoughts lie within these pages.

I am delighted to present *Fix Me*, a book that goes far beyond being a simple guide—it is an empowering journey that reveals the superhero within you. The title—*Fix Me*—may catch your attention, resonating with the desire for help and personal growth, often prompting individuals to seek therapy. However, it is essential to highlight that it is not an insult or a suggestion that you are broken. On the contrary, it signifies empowerment, emphasising that you have agency over your own life and possess the power to take positive steps towards personal growth and healing.

Fix Me serves as a roadmap, guiding you on the path to managing your mental and emotional well-being. This book takes an integrated and eclectic approach, encompassing both psychological and holistic perspectives. At the beginning of your journey, you will encounter a series of insightful quizzes designed to help you explore and understand your unique personal needs and whether this is the right book for you. Within its pages, you will find a wealth of knowledge, exploring the causes of anxiety while learning practical techniques for managing thoughts and emotions. Delving into the power of self-awareness, self-acceptance, and self-compassion, it will equip you to recognise your thoughts and sensations, enabling you to regain control and break free from distressing anxiety.

One important insight *Fix Me* offers is the significance of positive self-talk. Through practical exercises and techniques, you will learn to improve positive self-talk and nurture self-confidence. At the end of each chapter, you will discover the empowering *Fix Me* tools—resources designed to support and enhance your personal growth journey. These tools can be customised to suit your specific requirements, allowing you to pinpoint areas where additional support may be desired.

Throughout this transformative voyage, we will collaborate to deepen your self-understanding and develop effective coping mechanisms, enabling you to navigate life's challenges with greater ease and resilience. Let us embrace this expedition of self-discovery together and take the first step towards a more peaceful and fulfilling life. Remember, the title *Fix Me* symbolises your potential for growth and change. It does not imply that you are broken or in need of fixing. Instead, it serves as a testament to your innate strength and capacity to shape your own destiny.

With *Fix Me*, you can manage anxiety and embark on a journey of self-discovery. Change requires a mindset that desires it, and this book can help you achieve just that.

> **Please keep in mind that I am not a medical professional, and if you have been diagnosed with a severe illness such as psychosis or schizophrenia, it is crucial to seek further professional help, preferably from a clinical psychologist or psychiatrist.**

Throughout this book, we can work together to understand ourselves better, developing effective coping mechanisms to direct life's challenges with greater ease and resilience. So, let's embrace this journey of self-discovery together and take the first step towards a more peaceful and fulfilling life.

Is *Fix Me* the Right Book for You?

....

In order to make the most of your quest with *Fix Me*, it's essential to assess your mental health needs. This section aims to guide you through self-reflection by asking essential questions related to stress, coping mechanisms, learning preferences, and goals for mental well-being. By understanding your unique circumstances, you can tailor your approach to the book, making it a more personalised and practical resource for managing anxiety and achieving positive change. Take a moment to explore these questions and gain insight into your own mental health needs as you embark on this beautiful progressive journey.

Assessing Your Mental Health Needs

- Do you grapple with overwhelming stress and anxiety that leaves you feeling helpless and struggling to find relief?
- Are you seeking practical and effective tools to manage your emotions and thoughts, empowering yourself to take charge of your mental and emotional well-being?
- Do you desire to become, equipped with the knowledge and techniques to break free from anxiety and other forms of emotional distress?

If you answered "yes" to any of these questions, then *Fix Me* is the right book for you. With its comprehensive approach, this book offers practical advice and techniques to help you manage your emotions and thoughts and take control of your mental health.

Learning Style Preferences

- Do you have a passion for learning, and are you intrigued by uncovering the underlying causes of mental and emotional distress?
- Do you favour practical advice and step-by-step instructions, giving you actionable techniques to manage your thoughts and emotions?
- Are you drawn to personal stories and case studies that share the experiences of others as you navigate your own journey to better mental health?

Fix Me caters to different reader preferences by offering a balanced approach that includes a mix of research, practical advice, and personal anecdotes.

Coping Mechanisms and Support Systems

- Do you turn to exercise or mindfulness as healthy coping mechanisms to regulate your thoughts and emotions?
- Do you seek professional help from therapists or counsellors to receive expert guidance in managing your mental and emotional well-being?
- Do you look to self-help books or online resources to learn new techniques to manage your thoughts and emotions?
- Do you rely on medication or other coping mechanisms to seek relief from the burden of anxiety and stress?

By identifying your current coping mechanisms and support systems, you can better understand how *Fix Me* can supplement or enhance your existing techniques for managing anxiety.

Setting Goals for Mental Health

- Do you wish to reduce the frequency and intensity of anxiety attacks, manage your symptoms, and regain control over your thoughts and emotions?
- Are you looking to improve your overall mood and happiness, cultivating a positive outlook and a sense of contentment?
- Would you like to increase your self-awareness and self-confidence, building resilience and self-esteem to overcome life's challenges?
- Do you hope to learn to manage stress and anxiety long-term, developing the skills to cope with life's stresses and trials?

By identifying your goals for mental health, you can create a roadmap for how *Fix Me* can help you achieve them. In addition, the book provides practical advice and techniques to help you manage your thoughts and emotions and develop resilience and self-confidence.

Breaking Negative Patterns

- Are you struggling with unhealthy coping mechanisms, such as drinking, smoking, or overeating, that cause more harm than good to your mental and physical well-being?
- Do you find yourself avoiding situations that trigger your anxiety, limiting your experiences and opportunities for growth?
- Do you tend to ruminate and obsess over your anxious thoughts, creating a cycle of negative self-talk and self-doubt, where anxious thoughts consume your mind and leave you feeling helpless and overwhelmed?

If you answered "yes" to most of the quiz questions, then *Fix Me* is likely to be a valuable and helpful book for you to read. The quizzes are designed to assess different aspects of your mental health and well-being and to help you understand if you could benefit from the advice and techniques offered in the book. By answering "yes" to most of the questions, you have indicated that you are likely to benefit from the practical advice and techniques provided in the book, as well as the balanced approach that caters to different reader preferences.

Mental health is a complex and individualised experience, and it's essential to consider your own unique needs, preferences, and goals for mental health and well-being before deciding to read *Fix Me*. However, if you're struggling with stress and anxiety, looking to break free from negative patterns, and support resilience in the face of life's challenges, then *Fix Me* offers a comprehensive approach that can help you transform your mental and emotional health.

So, why wait? Explore the pages of *Fix Me* and discover how it can aid you to take control of your mental and emotional well-being and achieve your goals for a happier, healthier life. But before diving into the quick fixes in the next section for managing anxiety, it's important to acknowledge that everyone's journey is unique, and what works for one person may not work for another. However, these techniques have shown promising results for many individuals and can serve as helpful tools to navigate moments of distress. So, let's explore these practical strategies together and discover how they can provide you with a sense of relief and empowerment on your path to managing anxiety.

Quick Fixes for Managing Anxiety

It can be challenging to manage anxiety, but there are simple techniques you can use anywhere to help alleviate the symptoms. This section of the book provides seven quick fixes you can try, along with information about how they can help.

Grounding Techniques

If you're anxious, grounding techniques can help you feel more present and in control. Likewise, this technique is beneficial if you're experiencing racing thoughts or feeling overwhelmed. You can try any of these techniques.

- Focus on your senses. Touch different textures, smell different scents, listen to calming music, or look at a soothing image. This technique helps bring your focus back to the present moment and can help reduce feelings of stress or anxiety.
- Count backwards. Starting at a high number like 100, count backwards by 7s or any number you choose. This technique can be helpful if you're feeling overwhelmed or if your mind is racing.

- Use a grounding object. Hold onto a soothing object like a stress ball or a smooth rock. This technique can help bring your focus to the present and provide a sense of comfort and security.

Controlled Breathing

Breathing exercises are an effective way to manage anxiety. This practice can be helpful if you're experiencing physical anxiety symptoms like shortness of breath or a racing heart. Here's one quick method to try.

- Breathe from your diaphragm, take a deep breath through your nose, count to 5, and hold.
- Now, as you hold, count two.
- Take your time and exhale steadily through your mouth for a count of 5.
- Repeat the process for a few minutes until you feel calmer.

Mindfulness Meditation

Meditation can support you to focus on your thoughts and help you manage tension. (For a complete discussion of mindfulness, see Chapter 14.) This technique can be helpful if you're feeling overwhelmed or struggling with anxious thoughts. Here's a simple meditation technique you can try.

- Find a comfortable place to sit. It does not always have to be quiet.
- Feeling safe in your space, close your eyes, pause for a moment, and take a deep breath in and then out.
- Concentrate on your breath and observe your thoughts and feelings without judgement.
- If your mind drifts, gently bring your attention back to your breathing or focus on one object you can visualise and ask yourself questions until you feel calm, then focus on your breathing again.
- Continue to listen to your breathing, consciously trying to breathe from your diaphragm for a few minutes until you feel more relaxed.

Progressive Muscle Relaxation

This method involves tensing and relaxing muscle groups throughout your body to reduce tension and anxiety. This technique can be accommodating if you're experiencing physical anxiety symptoms like muscle tension or aches. Here's how to do it.

- Find an uninterrupted and comfortable place to lie down.
- Begin by focusing on your toes, tense the muscles in your feet for 5 seconds, then release.
- Move up your body, pulling and releasing each muscle group, including your legs, abdomen, arms, and face.
- Take a few deep breaths and let go, allowing your entire body to feel relaxed.
- You can also do this as a body scanning technique, focusing on every part of your body as you focus on each element.

Positive Self-Talk

Positive self-talk can significantly help you reframe unpleasant thoughts and reduce anxiety. This technique can be beneficial if you're struggling with negative self-talk or experiencing self-doubt. Here are some affirmations you can use.

- "I am calm and in control."
- "I can make good choices for myself."
- "I can handle this situation."
- "I trust myself and my abilities."
- "I choose to focus on positive thoughts."
- "I choose to take care of me."

Aromatherapy

Certain scents can help promote relaxation and reduce anxiety, making aromatherapy an excellent option for managing symptoms. The following essential oils are known for their calming properties.

- Lavender. This essential oil is perhaps the most popular for reducing anxiety and promoting relaxation. Its soothing scent can help improve sleep and reduce stress and tension; add a few drops to your pillow or tissue and place it near you.

- Bergamot. An essential oil known for its mood-lifting properties, it can help reduce stress and anxiety. It is also known to have a calming effect on the nervous system. Just place a few drops on a tissue and keep it near you.
- Frankincense. This essential oil is known for its grounding and centring properties, making it an ideal choice for those experiencing anxiety or stress. It can help calm the mind and promote inner peace.

If you're seeking anxiety relief, aromatherapy can be a practical option. First, add a few drops of essential oil to a diffuser and inhale the soothing scent. Next, mix with a carrier oil like coconut or almond oil and apply it topically (after ensuring the oil is safe for skin use, as indicated on the label). Follow recommended dilution rates and safety guidelines when working with essential oils.

Distract Yourself

Sometimes, distracting yourself from your anxious thoughts can help reduce anxiety. Here are some activities you can try.

- Immerse your face in a bowl of ice or wash your face in cold water. This activates the body's "diving reflex", slowing down the heart rate and promoting anxiety reduction.
- Participate in a hobby or creative activity that requires focus and concentration. This can include drawing, painting, knitting, or playing an instrument. Focusing on a creative task can help shift your thoughts away from anxious feelings and promote relaxation.
- Listen to music or a podcast that you enjoy. Music can have an immensely calming effect on the body and mind, and help reduce stress. So, choose uplifting music or podcasts, and listen whenever you need a quick distraction from anxious thoughts.
- Watch a funny video or movie. Laughter can be an effective way to reduce stress and anxiety. So, find a funny video or movie you

enjoy, and let yourself laugh and let go of your worries for a little while.

- Connect with a friend or loved one. Communication is essential; talking to someone you trust can help you handle your feelings and gain a new perspective. Talk to a friend or family member and share what you're going through. You might be surprised how much a listening ear can help you feel more comfortable.

Remember, managing anxiety is a process, and different techniques work for different people. Try other methods throughout the book to see what works best for you and be patient with yourself. You can cultivate peace and fulfilment by incorporating quick fixes into your daily routine and developing effective anxiety management techniques.

1

Anxiety Triggers

Having explored the quick fixes for managing anxiety, we now understand that true transformation and reclaiming our sense of peace require more than just simple techniques. Anxiety is a pervasive and debilitating experience that can leave us feeling helpless, overwhelmed, and alone. Many of us struggle with anxiety, asking ourselves "What is wrong with me?" or "How can I control these overpowering emotions?" If this resonates with you, know that you are not alone. As George Addair once said, "Everything you've ever wanted is sitting on the other side of fear." But how do we conquer this fear and regain our sense of peace and well-being?

This chapter explores the countless causes that lead to anxiety, which may surprise you as they can stem from almost anything. Anxiety can manifest in multiple ways, whether a single event, cumulative stress, or even something we are unaware of. As a therapist, I understand the profound impact that anxiety can have on our lives, and I empathise with those who are going through this emotional turmoil. Fear not; through my experiences, I will guide you through various exercises and techniques that have proven effective in managing anxiety.

It is essential to acknowledge that reading this book may sometimes trigger feelings of vulnerability and discomfort. If this happens, see Table 1.1: *List of Possible Anxiety Triggers* and test your anxiety levels. Of course, if you feel terrible, I urge you not to leave the book entirely and instead attend only to the sections that make you feel comfortable. You must be in the right mindset to engage with the techniques and exercises and apply them correctly. By doing so, you can transform the anxiety ailment you are battling. To do this, you must understand more about what sets you off.

As a social science psychology major turned educationalist, then psychotherapist, I have spent my career observing human behaviour methodically. Through personal experience, I have learned a lot about myself and others' responses to people, places, and events around us. However, according to a study conducted by developmental scientists at Harvard University, our powers of observation start from the day we are born and are geared outward, towards understanding and interpreting the responses of others rather than inward, towards reflecting on ourselves (Astington, 1993). This deprioritisation of self-reflection can significantly impact our mental health, limiting our ability to understand and navigate our emotional range and how it affects our relationships with others.

Understanding Your Motivations

What if we could learn to reflect on ourselves and cultivate substantial self-knowledge and emotional awareness? Doing so will allow us to better understand our needs, feelings, and desires without relying solely on external validation and reassurance, especially if we have anxiety. According to psychotherapist and researcher Dr Kristin Neff, cultivating self-compassion can lead to greater well-being and resilience (Neff, 2003).

Cultivating self-awareness and self-compassion is crucial for navigating life's challenges with any mental or emotional ailment. By understanding the complexities of life from the inside out, we can build a better relationship with ourselves and overcome the limitations of external validation. By reflecting on ourselves and developing solid self-knowledge, we can identify what triggers us, upsets us, or makes us anxious, and then learn to give ourselves the compassion we need to heal—emphasising the importance of treating ourselves with kindness, care, and understanding. In doing so, we can become more resilient, more emotionally aware, and more fulfilled in our relationships and life in general.

However, not everyone has access to therapy to facilitate this personal growth. I can relate to this first-hand. Growing up in the UK during the 1990s, therapy was not a common practice, and I was unaware of the benefits it could bring to my life. It wasn't until university that I heard the term "therapy" during a psychology lecture, and even then, I had no intention of becoming a therapist. Instead, my dream was to become a pilot, but my anxiety would not let me achieve that dream.

Whenever I was about to fly a plane, anxiety would show up, leaving me feeling debilitated and nauseous. It was not until my wise flying instructor pointed me towards self-exploration that I began to understand the root cause of my anxiety. He encouraged me to examine my mind and listen to my thoughts, hoping my rational mind would guide me. Reflecting on my inner triggers, I realised that my thoughts were far from reasonable. Nevertheless, I persevered, and through self-reflection and diligent research, mainly from books—as the internet was not readily accessible then— I could self-diagnose and take control of my emotions. By facing my fears head-on, I was empowered to rise above the overwhelming weight of anxiety which had held me back for far too long.

While I may not have been able to complete my private pilot licence (PPL) due to motion sickness, this transformative moment was a turning point in my life. It taught me to listen to my thoughts, acknowledge my fears, and understand that my responses to my anxious thoughts were always based on what others might think of me. I realised that I was overly judgemental of myself and feared that others in my environment might judge me too. Consequently, every time I attempted to do something, such as fly a plane, I felt the need to perform to an unattainably high standard, which was the main trigger for my anxiety and the onset of my physical symptoms of motion sickness.

Cultivating Self-Awareness

Understanding and cultivating self-awareness is a process that can lead to incredible personal growth and emotional resilience. By examining our thoughts, feelings, and behaviours, we can gain a greater understanding of ourselves and develop the necessary tools to navigate life's challenges with any mental or emotional ailment. This process of self-discovery requires effort and dedication, but the rewards of personal growth and relationship satisfaction are immeasurable. By becoming masters of our own emotional well-being, we can transform our relationship with ourselves and others.

As you read on, I know you understand that anxiety can be a debilitating experience, which can profoundly impact your daily life. The cycle of worry and amplification can exacerbate these feelings, leading to a vicious cycle that can be challenging to break free from. However, by developing emotional awareness and a better understanding of yourself, you can identify the sources of your anxiety and learn to manage your responses effectively. Effort and dedication can reduce anxiety and improve your overall mind. You can achieve a more fulfilling and meaningful life by taking charge of your emotional well-being.

Self-awareness and emotional regulation are vital to managing our mental and emotional well-being, and a crucial step in achieving this is identifying anxiety triggers. That's why I've compiled a comprehensive list of common anxiety triggers based on my professional experience and feedback from clients and referred patients. Each corresponding chapter in the book explores each trigger in-depth, providing practical exercises and techniques to manage them effectively, helping you transform your relationship with anxiety and live a fulfilling life.

To better understand anxiety, the next step is to take the trigger test. This assessment tool is designed to help you evaluate the anxiety you may feel by identifying the contributing factors. The test coincides with the book's chapters, providing an efficient way to understand anxiety and apply the techniques and tools provided. As you take the test, your thoughts and ideas about the book's context will help you understand your relationship with yourself first, allowing you to accept and apply what resonates with your self-care routine.

Remember, the title of this book is *Fix Me* for a reason—to help you take control of anxiety and start living the life you deserve. By embarking on this journey together, we can overcome anxiety one step at a time. If you experience any obstacles along the way, know that the practical exercises and techniques provided in the book will help you transform your relationship with anxiety and empower you to regain control (see Table 1.1).

Table 1.1 List of Possible Anxiety Triggers

Possible triggers	Measuring scale: 5 (feeling extremely anxious) to 1 (feeling extremely calm), write your number for each possible trigger below
Fear of public speaking	
Panic attacks and physical symptoms of anxiety	
Fear of failure and losing a job	
Feeling overwhelmed in crowded spaces	
Fear of flying and travel anxiety	
Grief and anxiety after the loss of a loved one or pet	
Fear of rejection and social anxiety	
Negative self-talk and self-sabotage	
Jealousy and comparison with others	
Difficulty communicating and maintaining healthy relationships	
Anxiety and panic in social situations	
Fear of bullying and traumatic experiences	
Fear of happiness	
Overthinking and difficulty with mindfulness	
Seeking natural remedies and alternative therapies for anxiety relief	
Total score	

The simple assessment tool of Table 1.1 is based on your score range, divided into three categories. If your score falls between 1 and 25, it suggests that you may not have any significant contributors to anxiety. However, if your score falls between 26 and 50, it indicates that you may have a few minor factors contributing to anxiety that you should be aware of and learn to manage effectively. Finally, if your score is between 51 and 75, significant factors may contribute to your anxiety, which requires further attention. In such cases, as well as using this book as a tool, you need to seek help from a mental health professional to help you identify and manage these factors before they negatively impact your quality of life. While seeking professional help becomes essential when our ability to manage anxiety is exhausted, books like this can serve as a valuable companion to therapy.

It's important to note that the reasons contributing to anxiety can change over time, and sometimes anxiety can be caused by a combination of internal and external factors. By understanding the issues contributing to anxiety, you can take steps to manage them and reduce their impact on your daily life. I recommend taking a pen and paper and noting other reasons contributing to anxiety to understand your condition better.

Managing anxiety can be challenging, but it's a road worth taking. With the right tools, techniques, and support, you can break free from anxiety spirals and live a life that embraces your strengths rather than constantly fighting against internal obstacles. It's essential to recognise that this book is designed to work alongside a therapist if anxiety is significant, and seeking professional help is crucial in such cases. In addition, it is essential to note that the factors contributing to anxiety may vary over time, highlighting the need to continuously work on our mental and emotional well-being to maintain a healthy and fulfilling life.

References

Astington, J. W. (1993). *The Child's Discovery of the Mind.* Cambridge, MA: Harvard University Press.

Neff, K. (2003). Self-compassion: An alternative conceptualisation of a healthy attitude toward oneself. *Self and Identity*, 2(2), 85–101.

2

The Feeling of Anxiety

....

In the previous chapter, I emphasised the importance of self-exploration to identify anxiety triggers and understand the emotional responses that often accompany them. Through this process of self-discovery, we can develop a deeper understanding of our inner workings and manage anxiety more effectively. The anxiety trigger exercise (Table 1.1) is a vital tool in this regard, as it allows you to score anxiety levels you feel on a scale of 1 (low) to 5 (high) and keep track of your progress as you work through the book. In this chapter, we will explore the countless feelings of anxiety and delve deeper into the complex emotions that often accompany them.

Anxiety can be a distressing experience, leading to further worry and potentially causing other mental and emotional ailments if left unaddressed. Understanding the sensations that arise when anxiety strikes are crucial to managing it effectively. While each type has unique characteristics, it is essential to recognise that the symptoms may vary from person to person. We will discuss physical symptoms in the next chapter.

So, what is this feeling of anxiety? The answer is not as simple as we would like it to be. Anxiety is a complex emotion that can cause further worry and make us feel like we are losing control. The fear of the unknown often overwhelms us, and our bodies react, generating emotions and physical symptoms. On occasion, we don't even know if it is anxiety that we are feeling.

To give you an idea about the complexities of anxiety, let me share a personal experience that helped me understand anxiety a little better. On 11 September 2001, a group of friends and I were in transition—a flight from Sardinia to London. Little did we know that on that day, the world would change forever due to the terrorist attacks on the Twin Towers in New York. The journey took much longer than expected, and we circled over England for some time. The cabin crew behaved oddly, and the captain didn't announce why we weren't landing. None of us, as passengers, had any idea what was happening, since we had no inflight internet or cell phone service.

The atmosphere in the cabin was eerie, burdening, and stressful. My friends and I picked up on the strange energy, and the cabin crew continued to disclose nothing. Instead, we overheard the cabin crew and other passengers guessing. One particular flight attendant kept patting her head and pacing, seeming agitated. She reassured everyone that all was well but seemed stressed, contradicting her statements. We grew increasingly nervous because of the crew's behaviour, and suddenly passengers were saying they felt sick and finding or requesting sick bags from the staff. Others were complaining about stomach aches and speculating about the food we had been served.

Despite not knowing what was happening, we recognised that something was wrong. Even though we couldn't identify the fear or the emotion at that moment, we knew we were uneasy. However, it wasn't until we could switch our phones back on once we landed that we realised what had happened that morning in New York.

The feeling of anxiety is incomprehensible until you can recognise it. By reviewing my most prevalent experiences in life, I now realise that miscarrying a baby meant I had no control over the future. When taken to the hospital, the uncertainty made me spiral into panic, feeling out of control, with a million questions pivoting in my mind about the future. I had a reason for my concern, I recognised I was anxious, but I only realised it because it was a familiar feeling. It is the same feeling we were all experiencing on that flight—fear, feeling out of control, and uncertainty about the future. We will explore the flight, fight, freeze, and other responses in Chapter 7.

Loss of Control

When anxiety strikes, feeling overwhelmed and out of control is natural. External events can trigger a cascade of disarray in our thoughts and physical reactions, just as they had when I was learning to fly. Recognising and identifying these sensations as a mixture of emotions and physical symptoms is crucial to effective management. Although attempting to rationalise our thoughts may be difficult, understanding the underlying emotions and their impact on our bodies is a significant first step in managing anxiety. By acknowledging our feelings and symptoms, we can control our anxiety response. It is possible to prevent it, and not always necessary to label it, although sometimes—once we identify the type and the symptoms—we can develop personalised strategies to treat it. However, people repeatedly get stuck when feeling anxiety and often lose control, feeling that there is no way out.

Managing anxiety can be challenging, but with the right tools, techniques, and support, it is possible to break free from its grip and embrace a life that amplifies our strengths rather than constantly battling internal obstacles.

Lisa Nichols shares her personal experiences and provides practical strategies to overcome challenges and create a life of fulfilment. As she wisely stated in her book, "Your thoughts and feelings determine your actions and the results you get. It all starts with your thoughts—and I have found that inspirational words are a quick way to retune your thinking." (Nichols, 2010)

The words of Lisa Nichols resonate deeply, reminding us of the immense power our thoughts hold and the significance of consciously selecting empowering words to reshape our mindset.

In the face of anxiety, it is crucial to acknowledge that this book serves as a valuable resource, but it should be complemented by the professional guidance of a therapist when anxiety becomes significant. The experience of feeling out of control or overwhelmed can be intimidating, and during such moments it is essential to focus on words that instil a sense of calm and empowerment within us. Moreover, it is important to recognise that the factors contributing to anxiety are dynamic, evolving over time. Thus, it becomes vital to continually invest in our mental and emotional well-being through self-care practices and personal growth, enabling us to lead a fulfilling life that prioritises our overall wellness.

Going back to the 9/11 story, when I was on the flight, the cabin crew attendant on the plane felt stuck and out of control while in transit. She knew there was nothing she could do to change her circumstances physically. Similarly, I felt out of control in my marriage and while trying for a baby, especially after losing the pregnancy. I was mired in uncertainty because there was nothing more I could do, and although it may seem illogical, I allowed anxiety to make me feel safe. I understood fear, but I did not understand the events of that day, so anxiety became a familiar and comfortable place for me to wait. This was also the case for all the passengers and crew on the flight. We were familiar with the anxiety feeling.

As I write this, I am reminded of the first time I experienced stage fright and felt utterly out of control. I was only eight years old, playing the role of one of the four Calling Birds in my school's Christmas play. I remember feeling a strange sensation in my body, and my stomach was in knots. It wasn't something I ate that caused this feeling; fear and nervousness were taking over me. I felt powerless in the face of the situation, and my palms were sweaty as my nerves got the better of me.

Most of what I remember from that day was the fear of someone hearing my stomach churning. I was embarrassed to be in front of my teachers and peers and worried about being judged. I felt so unstable that I froze and forgot my lines. I danced around the stage, flapping my arms when it wasn't my turn and twirling into other actors. Someone pushed me out of the way, and I knocked over others. To top it all off, the curtains fell on us. While the whole situation might have been comical, it was incredibly traumatising and embarrassing for a child my age.

Trauma and Anxiety

Childhood trauma and anxiety are closely linked due to the impact traumatic experiences can have on a child's developing brain and their ability to regulate emotions and respond to stress. Traumatic events disrupt the sense of safety, security, and predictability children need for healthy development. When children are exposed to chronic or severe stressors, their brains may adapt in ways that heighten their vulnerability to anxiety. This can lead to difficulties in regulating emotions and increased sensitivity to perceived threats or triggers.

As I matured and reflected on that particular experience, I came to the realisation that my fear extended beyond the mere act of performing. During that time, I was oblivious to the other significant events unfolding in my life. For instance, my father's illness had landed him in hospital, resulting in heightened anxiety and stress for me. It wasn't until later when I engaged in an activating exercise—an exercise that stimulates self-reflection and introspection—that I began to unravel the layers of my triggers and comprehend the multifaceted emotions attached to them. To "unpack" triggers and emotions means to delve deep into their underlying causes, examining and understanding them in detail. Through this process of exploration and introspection, I was able to gain insights into the various facets of my fears and emotions, allowing me to navigate them with greater clarity and self-awareness.

It is important to note that no matter how big or small the event, childhood trauma can contribute to the development of anxiety disorders later in life. This is because the traumatic experiences and the associated emotional and physiological responses can shape the individual's belief systems, perceptions of danger, and coping strategies. These can become deeply ingrained and persist into adulthood, leading to heightened anxiety symptoms and a predisposition to anxiety disorders.

As I delved deeper, I discovered that my fear of being in dark, enclosed spaces was triggered by an incident when I was only three years old. My uncle had deliberately locked me in a dark basement to stop me from crying, leaving a lasting impact on me. However, each time I looked back, I realised that there were more layers of emotions to unravel, and each trigger was tied to something else.

This shows that the experience of trauma can create a state of hypervigilance, where individuals remain on high alert, anticipating potential threats or dangers. This chronic state of anxiety can significantly impact one's ability to feel safe and secure, leading to heightened anxiety symptoms and difficulty managing stress.

It's important to note that not everyone who experiences childhood trauma will develop anxiety disorders, as individual resilience, support systems, and other factors also play a role. However, there is a strong association between childhood trauma and the increased risk of developing anxiety disorders in adulthood. Understanding this link can help inform therapeutic approaches and interventions to address the trauma and the resulting anxiety symptoms to promote healing and recovery.

Overall, it was a learning experience for me. By identifying my triggers and understanding the emotions tied to them, I better understood myself and how I reacted to certain situations. While confronting my fears and vulnerabilities wasn't always easy, it was an essential step towards personal growth and healing. This, in turn, helped me take control and regain my power.

The Roots of Anxiety

Okay, so let's say I unpacked the anxiety, but how do you identify it as the villain behind the emotion? It is identified by recognising its physical and emotional symptoms, such as restlessness, nervousness, rapid heart rate, sweating, and gastrointestinal problems. Emotional symptoms may include irritability, difficulty concentrating, and experiencing unwanted or intrusive thoughts. Panic attacks may also occur, which involve sudden and intense fear accompanied by physical symptoms such as chest pain. In extreme cases, anxiety might even mimic sensations of heart failure or stroke, causing difficulty breathing or severe chest pains. Recognising these emotional and physical symptoms can help identify anxiety as the underlying factor behind the overwhelming emotions. Seeking professional help is crucial if you experience any of these symptoms, due to anxiety's significant impact on our thoughts and overall well-being.

As an anxiety expert, I know—through working with my clients, referred patients, and my own journey—that anxiety can be complicated due to the prevalence of anxiety disorder symptoms. Anxiety disorders can manifest in various ways, leading to other conditions such as panic disorder, specific phobias, social anxiety disorder, agoraphobia, separation anxiety disorder, and illness anxiety disorder (hypochondria). These conditions can be acute or chronic, and affect a person's daily life and well-being. However, as a therapist, I utilise evidence-based methods to identify the root causes of these conditions and provide clients with practical solutions to manage and overcome their anxiety.

Through my personal observations and experiences in my profession, spanning over two decades, I have come to understand that anxiety is often intertwined with various conditions such as phobias, depression, and bipolar disorder, which involve extreme mood swings. While the exact cause of anxiety disorders remains unclear, researchers have identified stress, environmental factors, genetics, mindset, and anxiety itself as contributing factors. For instance, when I received a diagnosis of a potentially cancerous phyllodes tumour at a young age, I experienced heightened anxiety and questioned why this was happening to me. The consultant explained that stress, worry, environmental factors, and genetic predispositions can influence anxiety. While it may not have provided a fully satisfying answer, this underscored the intricate nature of anxiety disorders and the importance of tailored treatment approaches. In upcoming chapters, we will explore the cutting-edge research on fight-or-flight and other responses, and their implications for managing anxiety symptoms.

What triggers our reactive responses can be traced back to the intricate interplay among three critical regions of the brain: the amygdala, the hippocampus, and the prefrontal cortex. These brain structures are highlighted by LeDoux (2012) as playing critical roles in regulating our fear responses. The amygdala, a small, almond-shaped structure, holds particular significance in processing emotions, especially fear. The hippocampus, on the other hand, is responsible for learning, forming memories, and retrieving emotional memories. Meanwhile, the prefrontal cortex regulates emotions and decision-making processes (see Figure 2.1). These brain regions are interconnected and work in tandem to shape our fear responses and influence how we navigate and process emotional experiences. The arrows in Figure 2.1 indicate the flow of information and communication between these regions.

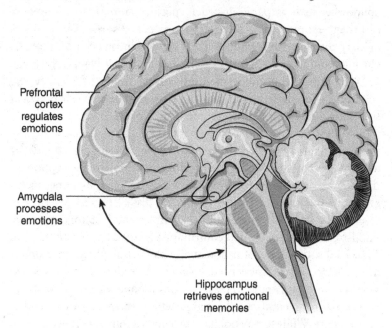

Prefrontal cortex regulates emotions

Amygdala processes emotions

Hippocampus retrieves emotional memories

Figure 2.1 Three Main Areas of Brain Function

These brain regions are integral parts of the sympathetic and autonomic nervous systems, which govern our bodily responses (Porges, 2007). Steven Porges was the creator of the polyvagal theory and explains its implications for understanding the autonomic nervous system, including the roles of the sympathetic and parasympathetic branches. He delves into the physiological mechanisms and functions of these branches and their influence on emotional regulation, social behaviour, and overall well-being.

Porges explains how, operating beneath conscious awareness, the autonomic nervous system controls essential bodily functions such as blood pressure, pupil dilation, heart rate, body temperature, and digestion. The external world and this central nervous system influence our experiences. Neurons (specialised nerve cells) orchestrate different physical reactions, including the actions of the skeletal muscles. Through this intricate process, individuals can find themselves caught in a cycle of physiological responses. The sympathetic nervous system, responsible for the body's rapid, involuntary responses to danger or stress, triggers heightened heart rate, increased stress levels, accelerated breathing, and more. Reading about this research resonated with me, reminding me of the shared response we felt during our return flight from Sardinia on September 11th.

Once the body recognises the physical symptoms associated with anxiety, the mental, emotional, and physical distress can become challenging to manage. In such instances, we must work with the tools available to us, and our mind is the most powerful tool at our disposal. It is essential to explore our coping mechanisms and the ways in which we approach anxiety. As a child, I would often cry due to the overwhelming anxiety I felt, primarily manifested in my gut as an instinctive response. It is worth noting that the human small intestine houses nearly 100 million neurons, and as a child it is understandable that exams, stage fright, spiders, or other triggers would wind me up. My older brother, Jazz, would often tell me to "get a grip", and I now comprehend the wisdom of his words. Slowing down those racing thoughts and finding a sense of inner stability can be invaluable in navigating anxiety's challenges.

In light of my personal journey and insights, it becomes evident that anxiety is intricately linked to various mental health conditions. While the precise causes of anxiety disorders remain elusive, researchers have identified numerous contributing factors. Notably, the amygdala, hippocampus, and prefrontal cortex—crucial brain regions involved in fear regulation—illuminate the underlying neural mechanisms of anxiety (LeDoux, 2012). Moreover, comprehending the dynamic interplay between our external environment and the autonomic nervous system, encompassing both the sympathetic and parasympathetic branches, offers valuable insights into the physiological responses associated with anxiety (Porges, 2007). By cultivating self-awareness and acquiring effective coping strategies, you can gain greater agency in managing anxiety and fostering emotional well-being. It is vital to recognise the significance of seeking professional help and support, as therapists can provide tailored guidance for addressing significant anxiety.

Therefore, managing anxiety can be challenging, but it is possible to slow down the internal processes of the body and mind. The parasympathetic nervous system plays a crucial role in this process by acting as a brake, slowing down the organs once it realises the body is not in danger (see Chapter 7). In addition, it triggers the "rest and digest" response, also known as the relaxation response, which can help reduce anxiety symptoms immediately. You can lift your mood, lower your blood pressure, and improve your immunity by activating the parasympathetic nervous system. The encouraging thing about this book is that it offers quick fixes at the beginning and techniques throughout, so with regular practice you can avoid spiralling into chaos or anxiety panic—the body can learn to control its responses better.

In Chapter 1, I briefly shared how I wanted to be a pilot and could not continue due to motion sickness. Well, a part of my journey also led me to do parachute jumps, and it is because of this that I wish to share an analogy to help you start processing how the feeling of anxiety works. Jumping out of a plane with a parachute can be related to the parasympathetic nervous system response. Just as a parachute slows a fall, so the parasympathetic nervous system slows down the body's response to stress and anxiety. However, like jumping out of a plane, activating the parasympathetic response can feel like taking a risk, especially when you are facing intense emotional or mental turmoil.

Anxiety can be an unwelcome and ever-present enemy, making it challenging to identify and manage. When caught up in an anxious state, an overflow of chemicals and hormones such as cortisol can lead to negative responses, leaving you stuck and unable to manage the anxiety you may feel. However, you can learn to take control of anxiety by making the parasympathetic response automatic, even during mental and emotional chaos.

The "mindful" part of the brain has a pause button that allows you to slow down and assess the situation, just like the pause before jumping out of a plane. By focusing on the present and changing your perspective, you can reassess your thoughts in a way that helps you take control. This ability can be used to handle intense worrying or fearful situations, empowering you to approach problems with a more positive and productive mindset. With practice, you can learn to activate the parasympathetic response just like a parachute slows down a fall, providing safety and control in even the most challenging circumstances.

Learning how to retrain your brain to take control of your thoughts and emotions can significantly improve your quality of life. For example, anxiety, worry, and fear are learned behaviours that can take over your life and affect your ability to enjoy each day. However, with the proper techniques and exercises, you can learn how to manage these emotions and gain control over your thoughts.

Fix Me Tools

Know Yourself. Understanding when anxiety, worry, and fear are present is crucial in controlling these emotions. Keeping a journal to record when you have a fearful thought and when the thinking takes place can help you understand yourself better. In addition, you can slowly learn more about yourself by setting easy, realistic, and achievable goals for facing worry, anxiety, or fear. Developing a list of things that help you when you are likely to become frightened can also be beneficial. Great tools like listening to positive and uplifting podcasts. Reading books you enjoy will also help.

Move and Exercise. Exercise is a proven method for significantly reducing anxiety, worry, and fear. Starting with simple exercises and slowly increasing the amount of daily activity can help take your mind off your concerns. Any form of movement is good for you, and it requires some concentration, which can take your mind off your worries.

Learn to Relax. Relaxation techniques can help ease the mental, emotional, and physical pain associated with anxiety, worry, and fear. Proper breathing techniques can be found throughout the book, and meditation can be an excellent tool for diverting your attention from the things that are bothering you. By focusing your thoughts and concentrating on something other than your fears, you can distract yourself from anxiety and achieve a state of calm.

Change Habits. Changing the habits that have not helped you in the past is essential in managing anxiety, worry, and fear. Eating lots of fruit and vegetables and avoiding too much sugar and caffeine (and for some people, avoiding alcohol) can significantly reduce anxiety. Everything should be in moderation, and alcohol's after-effects can often make you feel worse. Changing habits can be challenging, but it's a crucial step in managing anxiety and taking control of your thoughts. By practising these techniques and exercises, you can learn to manage anxiety, worry, and fear, and gain control over your thoughts and emotions. It's essential to remember that anxiety is a learned behaviour, and with the right tools you can change these thought patterns and take control of your life.

At the beginning of this chapter, I said we would look at the various types of anxiety. So please see the following:

- *Generalised anxiety disorder (GAD).* Excessive and persistent worrying about everyday events or activities.
- *Panic disorder.* Sudden and unforeseen panic attacks that can cause physical symptoms, for example heart palpitations, sweating, and shortness of breath.
- *Social anxiety disorder (SAD).* Fear of social and performance situations, where individuals fear being judged or scrutinised by others.
- *Obsessive–compulsive disorder (OCD).* Recurrent and intrusive thoughts or images (obsessions) that lead to repetitive behaviours or mental acts (compulsions) to alleviate anxiety.
- *Post-traumatic stress disorder (PTSD).* A response to experiencing or witnessing a traumatic event that can cause flashbacks, nightmares, and severe anxiety symptoms.

- *Specific phobia.* A fear of a particular object or situation, such as spiders or heights, which can cause extreme anxiety and avoidance behaviour.
- *Separation anxiety disorder.* Excessive anxiety where being disconnected from a person or place presents feelings of insecurity.
- *Agoraphobia.* A fear of being in places or circumstances where escape may be intricate or help may not be available, such as crowded areas or public transportation.
- *Illness anxiety disorder.* Previously known as hypochondria, this disorder is defined by excessive fear and worry about serious illness.
- *Body dysmorphic disorder (BDD).* A preoccupation with perceived flaws or defects in one's appearance that causes significant distress and impairment.
- *Hoarding disorder.* A difficulty in discarding possessions, regardless of their actual value, that results in cluttered living spaces and functional impairment.
- *Trichotillomania.* A recurrent urge to pull out your own hair, resulting in hair loss and significant distress or impairment.
- *Excoriation disorder.* A recurrent habit of picking at your own skin, resulting in skin lesions and significant distress or impairment.
- *Generalised anxiety and depression.* This is a combination of anxiety and depression that can cause pervasive and persistent worry, sadness, and loss of interest in activities and life in general.
- *Adjustment disorder with anxiety.* A reaction to a stressful life event that causes significant anxiety symptoms.
- *Substance/medication-induced anxiety disorder.* Anxiety symptoms can be caused by substance use or medication.
- *Anxiety disorder.* Anxiety symptoms caused by a medical condition.
- *Unspecified anxiety disorder.* Symptoms of anxiety that are causing significant distress but do not meet the criteria for a specific anxiety disorder.
- *High-functioning anxiety.* A type of anxiety characterised by persistent worry and fear, often manifesting as perfectionism,

overwork, and excessive planning, while maintaining a high functioning level in daily life.

It's important to note that these are a number of anxiety disorders, but there are more, and anxiety disorders can be complex and overlap with other mental health conditions, so seeking professional support with a combination of therapy options can provide an effective treatment plan.

References

LeDoux, J. (2012). Rethinking the emotional brain. *Neuron*, 73(4), 653–676.

Nichols, L. (2010). *No Matter What!: 9 Steps to Living the Life You Love.* Piatkus.

Porges, S. W. (2007). The polyvagal perspective. *Biological Psychology*, 74(2), 116–143.

3

Physical Symptoms of Anxiety

···

This chapter delves deeper into the physical symptoms of anxiety, following the foundational discussions in Chapters 1 and 2. It explores the impact of anxiety on physical health, highlighting the importance of distinguishing between acute and chronic pain. Acute pain has a known source and an expected time to end, while chronic pain which can be caused by various physical, psychological, and neurological factors is consistent and often without an expected end date. Chronic pain is associated with other mental effects such as depression, anger, anxiety, stress, and sometimes a loss of sexual desire, and it often accompanies a disability or a permanent or semi-permanent reduction in mobility (Columbia University, 2022). This chapter encourages readers to acknowledge the intricate connection between physical and mental health and seek a comprehensive pain management approach.

According to Columbia University's study, approximately 25% of individuals who suffer from chronic pain will be diagnosed with chronic pain syndrome (CPS). The combination of chronic pain and other long-term mental effects like anxiety and depression characterises CPS. In addition, CPS can occur in individuals who experience other long-term pain conditions such as fibromyalgia, fatigue syndrome, endometriosis, inflammatory bowel disease, and post-stroke patients. This highlights the significant impact of chronic pain on mental health and the need for comprehensive treatment approaches that address both the physical and mental aspects of chronic pain management.

Living with chronic pain can be a complex and challenging experience, and even specialists struggle to understand its causes, let alone find a cure. While it's not possible to list all the physical symptoms associated with chronic pain, it's essential to recognise that it's a real and often debilitating condition. It's important to differentiate between occasional headaches or muscle cramps and chronic pain, which lasts for months or even years. If you're unsure about the nature of your pain, seeking medical attention is always advisable. To illustrate the impact of chronic pain, let me share the story of two clients with vastly different experiences. Despite their different backgrounds and symptoms, both found they had more power over their condition than initially thought.

The Issue of Chronic Pain

Allow me to share a touching story about two individuals, Jas and Pips, whose experiences illustrate our power in managing chronic pain. To protect their privacy, these names are aliases. Jas and Pips hail from different corners of the world and had different upbringings and medical histories, except for one shared affliction—Sjogren's syndrome. This chronic autoimmune disorder is characterised by an immune system attacking and damaging the body's moisture-producing glands, leading to chronic dryness in the eyes, mouth, and other mucous membranes. It is accompanied by symptoms such as exhaustion, joint pain, and swelling, which can impact one's quality of life. I understand that there is no cure for Sjogren's syndrome. Various treatments, such as medications and lifestyle changes, can aid in symptom management and improve overall well-being.

Jas and Pips share an almost identical symptom of dryness in various parts of their bodies, such as their mouth, eyes, and skin.

The similarities end there, as they come from different backgrounds and have had varied life experiences. When Jas reached out to me, it was through her mother, while Pips contacted me independently. I treated both clients using the eclectic approach in psychology, which means drawing from multiple therapy approaches and selecting the best treatment for individual clients. Through this process, I learned that despite their differing histories, they shared the same condition and experienced adversity and life's stresses in their own unique ways. However, their past experiences with anxiety differed. Jas had experienced the loss of her father and had neglected her physical health, resorting to unhealthy lifestyle choices, such as indulging in sugar, alcohol, and smoking. Pips, on the other hand, was content and happy with her past experiences, and chose to lead a consciously healthy lifestyle by changing her diet and making other lifestyle changes.

When addressing their chronic pain, the two clients' paths diverged. Jas decided not to continue treatment for her anxiety, as she believed nothing could be done for her Sjogren's syndrome, and her list of symptoms only worsened with time. Her anxiety levels increased whenever she thought of the debilitating consequences of her condition, and she did not wish to continue with therapy. Conversely, Pips took her mental health seriously and viewed it as vital to her physical health. With the tools I provided, such as personalised relaxation recordings (which Pips listened to for at least 66 days), she was able to form new habits to support her overall well-being. She made every effort to let go of what was holding her back, changed her diet, and prioritised exercise, recognising that endorphins play a significant role in chronic pain management. Today, Pips copes with her condition much better than Jas, both physically and mentally. This example highlights our power in managing our chronic pain and the importance of taking control of our well-being.

Through my independent case studies, it has become apparent that anxiety and chronic pain are often interconnected. While the connection is not fully understood, research suggests that anxiety can worsen chronic pain symptoms and impact our perception of pain. Anxiety can activate the body's stress response, increasing inflammation and pain sensitivity. Anxiety can also affect how we interpret and cope with pain, creating a negative cycle of increased anxiety and pain. Managing anxiety and pain symptoms is essential in improving one's overall well-being.

So, what are the most common physical symptoms related to anxiety? Please remember that this is not an exhaustive checklist if you are anything like I used to be, you will tick them all. And experiencing one or more of these symptoms does not necessarily mean you have anxiety. However, being aware of them is essential, as they can often be connected to anxiety and other conditions:

- Nebulous stomach ache
- Gastrointestinal distress
- Hyperventilation (overbreathing)
- Tension
- Trouble concentrating
- Itching/allergies
- Dizziness
- Tiredness
- Palpitations (fast beating, fluttering, or pounding of the heart)
- Muscle aches and tension
- Trembling and shaking
- Dry mouth
- Excessive sweating
- Shortness of breath
- Feeling sick
- Pins and needles (tingling sensations)
- Fatigue
- Chest pain
- Insomnia or sleep difficulties
- Breathing difficulties
- Headaches

Headaches, in particular, are one of the most common physical symptoms my clients mention. However, it's important to note that they can have various causes, including anxiety, and should be evaluated by a healthcare professional. If you experience any physical symptoms, please be kind to yourself and seek medical attention if needed. Remember, experiencing physical symptoms related to anxiety does not make you weak or broken; it's a normal human response to stress and can be managed with proper care and attention.

Experiencing physical symptoms of anxiety can be challenging and confusing, and seeking information online can often make things worse. The internet is full of possibilities, some of which may inform you that your symptoms indicate a severe medical condition, causing unnecessary panic and anxiety. Falling into this trap is easy, as I can attest to personally. My own experience with anxiety and physical symptoms of headaches was so severe at times that I was convinced death was near. To make matters worse, my anxiety was fuelled by the fact that my father had died of a brain haemorrhage, which gave my anxiety plenty of fodder to work with. In such a situation, you must remind yourself that not everything you read online is accurate or relevant to your circumstances. By recognising the potential pitfalls of "Dr Google" and acknowledging your own experiences and emotions, you can take a more measured approach to managing anxiety-related physical symptoms.

I understand that it can be challenging to control physical symptoms that trigger anxiety, which can lead to feeling out of control. Anxiety works like a robotic vacuum, constantly searching for something to pull up and bring your thoughts to the forefront. Even a normal headache or doctor's visit can become an opportunity for anxiety to take control. I vividly remember my first experience with a migraine, which unsettled me because of my past context. I believed my head was about to explode, and the junior doctor on duty asked me a typical question about family history of headaches. When I told him about my father's death from a "headache", the doctor's reaction startled me. However, the reality was that the anxiety in my mind changed my perception of the question, not the doctor's response. Therefore, it's crucial to understand how anxiety can affect our perception and thoughts and take control of this to avoid further negative consequences.

Despite our best efforts, certain events in life are beyond our control. These events can create anxiety and distress, as we struggle to cope with the uncertainty and fear they bring. Whether it is a loved one's illness or an unexpected accident, anxiety can find something to latch onto and exacerbate. As someone who has experienced this first-hand, I understand the profound impact such events can have on our mental and emotional well-being. In my darkest moments, I bordered on hypochondria, constantly searching for signs of illness and fearing the worst. I have seen this behaviour in many of my clients, and it is clear that we all have reasons for feeling anxious. However, it is essential to remember that we cannot control everything in life, and learning to manage anxiety in these situations can significantly improve our overall well-being.

Our mental and physical well-being are interconnected, and our mental state can influence our perception of ourselves and our conditions. Do you recall how I spoke in Chapter 2 of unpacking the anxiety? Anxiety can impact how we interpret information and react to it, potentially leading to physical symptoms. While chronic pain and illness are genuine and cannot be ignored, it is crucial to understand how anxiety can exacerbate these conditions. Well, the way we approach and manage these challenges can determine the extent to which anxiety impacts our physical health. Therefore, addressing and managing anxiety to prevent further physical effects and promote holistic well-being is essential.

Chronic pain can be intensified by anxiety and fear, as emotional responses triggered by these feelings recall past experiences of pain. The brain responds by bringing these memories to the surface, intensifying pain sensations. Anxiety is a natural response of the body to protect us from perceived danger, but in the case of chronic pain, this response is not always necessary. The mind does not differentiate between reality and vivid imagination, and the body responds to the mind's fear like it would to a real threat. Memories and emotions related to past experiences of pain can fuel anxiety and trigger physical symptoms, such as rapid breathing and hyperventilation.

Managing Anxiety Due to Pain

The brain does not distinguish between reality and frightening memories, and the body reacts similarly. Therefore, distraction is highly effective for managing anxiety and chronic pain. The distraction allows you to feel in control again, and it is a valid technique that works for most people. In addition, focusing on other activities or things that can take your mind off the pain or anxiety can reduce the intensity of pain and anxiety, making it more manageable.

Clients often express concerns about their ability to manage the physical symptoms of anxiety, but it is possible to control them. Although moving away from thoughts of pain can be challenging, it is not impossible. Pain is a significant trigger for anxiety, and managing the mind is essential to prevent anxiety from returning to it. Distracting the mind through breathing exercises, conversation, or other activities can minimise the impact of anxiety. It's important to remember that the pain is real and valid, but it can be managed with the right tools and techniques. Taking control of your mind can prevent anxiety from exacerbating your physical symptoms.

I've seen this in multiple clients. I had a client, Amrit, who suffered from chronic pain. In a troubled state one night, she called to tell me that she was enduring constant pain even after taking medication and painkillers to suppress it. In this situation, the pain was being chewed on constantly by anxiety. The pain wouldn't go away because her mind was stuck on it. Her fear of the pain only made her actual pain even worse.

We applied distraction and mindfulness techniques to pull her out of this cycle. First, I distracted her by discussing the different types of available breathing techniques and their impact on her mind and body. Then, after she calmed down, she was fascinated and commented that she had only just realised that her pain tended not to be present when she focused on something else, like cooking.

When it comes to pain, acute pain is only one type, while chronic pain can be a constant presence, particularly with certain disorders. The difficulty in diagnosing, treating, and recovering from chronic pain makes managing it even more challenging. The pain can feed into a cycle of anxiety and worry, worsening the situation. To break this cycle, distraction is key. Breathing exercises, exercise, hobbies, or grounding techniques can all help to take the mind away from the pain and focus it on something else.

This creates more space to manage the pain and allows for a new normal to be established. With practice, distracting yourself can become an empowering habit, allowing for better chronic pain management.

The distraction technique can be anything that works for you. Don't judge yourself—just use what works. One prevalent research-based practice that I frequently use with my clients is to root their thoughts in the physical environment around them. I call this the *grounding* technique. I usually begin by asking random questions to help the client feel grounded. What does this mean? When I say grounded, I mean in control, level-headed, and present. For example, I might ask things like "Where are you? Are you alone or with someone? Can you hear anything apart from my voice? Is there a particular smell? Do you feel comfortable where you are? Are you safe?"

Grounding techniques are effective in managing the physical symptoms of anxiety and pain. These techniques involve focusing on something comforting or engaging in a breathing exercise to draw attention away from the discomfort of the pain and help control thoughts and emotions. Research has shown that grounding techniques can reduce pain intensity and improve mood in individuals with chronic pain conditions. To effectively use grounding techniques, you create a list of questions or prompts that bring you into the present moment and can be used in various situations. By practising grounding techniques regularly, you can develop the skill of managing physical symptoms and reducing the impact of anxiety on your daily life.

One of the best examples of effective distraction in action I have ever seen was many years ago, when I was teaching in an old Victorian primary school with a cement playground surface. The children enjoyed kicking a football around at playtime. One day I was a part of the leadership staff on duty, and my class was playing too roughly. A child tripped another classmate, and I heard some children shouting. Joe, the boy who'd been tripped, was lying on the ground. I almost flew across the playground and was immediately devastated. It was apparent that this was a severe injury, not just the usual playground mishap. I could see the end of a bone poking out of his thigh, but thankfully it had not ripped through his skin.

I felt nauseous. The intense need to vomit was overwhelming. However, I needed to be present to help this child, who was in enormous pain. I focused on the current event and fought back the anxiety, blowing the whistle while other staff took over to clear the playground. I had to control my physical symptoms and desire to flee and vomit, modify the flight-and-fight response, and try to ground myself. I also had to ensure Joe's safety.

Joe lay there, looking very small. He confirmed that he had fallen, and I asked all the usual first-aid questions. Finally, Joe was conscious, ready to get up, and even tried to move his shoulders. But I insisted he lay still. I said absolutely nothing to him about his injury. My main fear was that I might exacerbate his undiagnosed injury if I disturbed him in any way. The femur bone poking the skin in front of his thigh was bad enough I certainly didn't want to make anything worse. He admitted that his leg hurt, but said he felt "fine". This is common with acute injury as well. The body goes into shock and refuses to process the level of pain present immediately.

Joe, the teaching assistant from the school, and I chatted calmly about football. I now know it was for about five or ten minutes, but honestly, it felt like half a lifetime. Finally, we had it under control. Joe was still sniffling and saying his leg was hurting and wanted to move. He was also a little tearful and wanted his mum. I mean, the poor kid was only ten. He had no clue he had broken his bone. The teaching assistant and I continued diverting his attention from the pain. We told Joe that his mother would arrive soon, and the paramedics would take him to hospital.

Joe's mother arrived about the same time as the paramedics. Fearing for her child, and seeing him in that terrifying state, she did the worst thing possible—she screamed. Her shocked reaction triggered a fear-filled response in her son, and in response, the boy trembled, shook violently, and blacked out!

His physical response was only a reaction to his mother's out-of-control screaming. Not to the pain. Until his mother and the ambulance arrived, his pain had been under control. But he lost control when he saw the panic in his mother's eyes. When Joe heard his mother's frightened scream, his thoughts about the pain, the horror of being told that the bone was broken, as it lifted the skin, and his anxiety over wanting to move and escape led his fear to take over. The response of his breathing led to hyperventilation, which led to him blacking out.

Are the anxiety and pain real? Despite the incident about Joe being genuine, there are occasions when people question if anxiety and pain are real. I want to reassure you that anxiety and pain *exist*. They are real and valid. However, there are also situations in which anxiety can take a perfectly normal situation and expand upon it until it feels abnormal—when it is actually still normal. For instance, when someone is watching the news about a disease, they can begin to believe they have similar symptoms. It is common to create ideas and thoughts that the symptoms are occurring to you when you hear about them. This, in turn, can make you worry and feel anxious.

I recall being with a friend when we first heard about COVID-19. The newsreader described the coronavirus in terrifying terms and highlighted all the symptoms. While watching the news, my friend announced that she had it. She was adamant about it. She'd had none of the symptoms before she heard them described. However, the more she watched the news, the more she believed she had COVID. Thankfully, she has never contracted the virus; her fear was real, but the symptoms weren't.

Trying to convince someone in opposition to what they've created in their own mind will make you realise that they simply cannot believe you because of the concerns that their anxiety has developed. It's just one more way that worries can change your life, usually not for the better.

Let's return to Joe, the injured child. This accident had a far more worrying corollary. He became anxious even after he made a full recovery. Why? Because unintentionally, his mother had instilled in him the fear of breaking his leg again. It took a long time, but with much encouragement and support, Joe returned to playing football several months later. One of the key factors in this was a physiotherapist who insisted that he continue to play sports to strengthen his leg.

The events of the past had a negative impact on the present. Joe's mother feared the worst. Her anxiety influenced him, resulting in him developing anxiety himself. The worry and learned behaviour made him think he might break his leg again. So, even after he returned to the playground, fully recovered, he would say that his leg hurt. Supported by the physio and physical education coaches, he was finally convinced that it was safe to play football again. They recreated and recalled his many happy memories of playing, and that it was a safe and fun thing for him to do. Anxiety and pain are real. They're valid and they can influence each other. By recognising how anxiety and pain interact, we can more effectively control and work with our pain.

Most people occasionally experience anxiety. As we have learned, anxiety is a *normal* response to a threat. However, if you have picked up this book, you may suffer from more than occasional anxiety. The anxiety may be closer to becoming a disorder.

An anxiety disorder is when normal anxiety interferes with our ability to function, triggers emotions, and creates uncontrolled reactions, like chronic pain. For example, being nervous about taking an exam is a typical expression of anxiety. Feeling like you're going to vomit every time you hear the word "exam" is an anxiety *disorder*. Fear can become a condition if it continues uncontrolled for a long time. However, in many cases, you can control the anxiety *before* it becomes a disorder. If you feel like you are experiencing anxiety symptoms that affect your physical or emotional health, or just make everyday life difficult, some of your anxiety has likely developed into a disorder. In that case, asking your GP or primary care provider to rule out medical issues that cause the same symptoms is a good idea. Once you get the physical all-clear from your doctor, you know that you can work on your mental health.

There is no comprehensive test for anxiety disorders, but there are many helpful questions to discuss and reflect on to diagnose them. Unfortunately, there is no one-size-fits-all treatment when it comes to anxiety. Being in physical and emotional pain is like carrying heavy baggage. I suggest that whatever you are experiencing, you should not dismiss it.

Fix Me Tools

Practice Acceptance. This is crucial for effectively managing and disciplining your emotions towards pain. It involves acknowledging the existence of pain and accepting it as a present reality. Once you accept its presence, you can focus on finding constructive ways to deal with it that work effectively for you. Sometimes, a simple change in routine or environment can serve as a necessary distraction from the pain. For instance, taking a short break to relax your body when it's tired, even if it's just for five minutes, can make a difference. Engaging in activities like washing your hands or combing your hair during a bathroom break can also provide a helpful distraction. Going for a gentle walk and changing your physical surroundings can also be beneficial. The key is to keep moving and distract yourself enough to overcome the difficult moment.

Acceptance is a progressive process that involves acknowledging and addressing your feelings while ensuring that your physical and emotional needs are balanced. It's important not to hesitate in seeking support from your family and friends. Having practical and emotional support can provide you with a sense of contentment and security during challenging times.

By embracing acceptance, you can reduce pain, increase inner peace, alleviate anxiety, and develop better coping mechanisms. Neuro-linguistic programming (NLP) techniques can be a valuable tool in this process (Kandola, 2017). NLP involves understanding that pain sometimes subsides and creating "anchors" to a pain-free state, which can be triggered when you need a boost. This type of treatment may also assist you in discovering new methods to manage and overcome pain.

Deal With Negative Thoughts. It is easy to spiral into a whirlwind of hopelessness. I understand this entirely, as each time I miscarried or the IVF treatment did not work, I felt devastated and depressed. It is too easy to fall into frustration or the victim mentality because you think there is no control or justification.

My ex-husband and I may have blamed each other during my difficult time. It is important to remember that some things are just not under your control. Allow yourself to feel the uncomfortable emotions and process them—but don't get mired in them or, even worse for your potentially happier future, wallow in them. You can take your information and communicate your concerns assertively (if necessary) to health professionals, who can give you practical pain management information.

You decide whether you want to triumph over the pain or make it your friend and learn from it. Or if you will be a victim and have it take over your life. Your pain is no one else's problem but your own.

The nurse treating me at the clinic after the miscarriage could see that my ex and I were not so responsive to each other. She once said, "No one cares about the pain someone else goes through" and while that might sound callous, I did learn something important from it. Everyone experiences their own pain, whether this is physical or emotional. I was not the only one suffering, my ex was too, albeit emotionally. But I had to care for myself because I felt both physical and emotional pain. I could look to others for support, but I had to take possession of helping myself. My ex was aware of this. He said it a few times to me I could do my best by moving away from the negative thoughts that accompanied the pain, but I could not cope at the time, to be honest I did not know how to back then. He eventually had had enough and walked away from us, as this was the best way he knew to cope with the pain.

Pace yourself, your emotions, your activities, and your lifestyle. It is highly desirable to maintain your motivation and forward momentum. It is much easier to deal with fears and obstacles along the way than when you've been sitting with them for too long.

Be Mindful of the Pain. Be aware of the pain, but don't let it control you. If you ignore the pain, the mind will play tricks on you. You're aware it is there, of course. Certain types of pain can become obsessive, just as with Jas and her Sjogren's syndrome. She was unwilling to focus on the present or any solutions to deal with the chronic pain. In comparison, remember the boy Joe, with the broken leg? He knew that he'd had an accident. This was acute pain, but he didn't allow the pain to control him—instead, he allowed us to distract him. His mother naturally allowed her fear to take ownership, but Joe didn't. He knew about the accident but didn't allow it to dominate his thoughts initially. Nor did he allow it to hinder his future; as I recently heard, he now plays football professionally for a local team.

If we allow ourselves to fall into the trap of letting pain be our master, we aggravate it. In Joe's situation, that would have meant the deprivation of playing football, which he loved. Know or learn what works for you to move away from pain. A balanced approach, with paced activity or distraction from undue aggravation of the pain, is best.

Take a Nap. If it tires you, take a nap. We often feel guilty for sleeping when we are unwell. And as many of us have experienced, just before we should be going to sleep, we can become anxious or irritable about our inability to sleep peacefully. So, if you can have a relaxing nap, just take one—without the guilt!

There are also things you can do to get better sleep, including

- Meditating
- Listening to music
- Relaxing before bed
- Taking a warm bath
- Playing a favourite relaxation video
- Practising or learning self-hypnosis
- Using supplements
- Using essential oils

Don't overlook the obvious things. For example, ensure you have a comfortable mattress, bedding, and a restful room temperature.

There are some excellent books on sleep; if the pain is preventing you from sleeping, then acquire one of these.

Pain and chronic pain are genuine and valid and can be a great source of anxiety. Hopefully, in this chapter, you have learnt some ways to manage and deal with acute or chronic pain. No matter what, be gentle and forgiving of yourself. You are worth the compassion you would extend to others, which also applies to your pain.

References

Columbia University (2022). *Chronic Pain Syndrome (CPS)*. Retrieved from https://www.columbia.edu/chronic-pain-syndrome.

Kandola, R. (2017). Neuro-linguistic programming (NLP) techniques for chronic pain. *British Journal of Pain*, 11(1), 49–55.

4

Three Brains Equilibrium (3BE)

This chapter explores the fascinating connection between the mind and body. In the preceding chapter, you discovered that your mind could influence pain intensity by dialling it up or down. You also learned that anxiety is often used to amplify the effects of pain when your mind turns up the volume. However, anxiety can become a disorder if left unchecked, significantly impacting your life.

Let's take a closer look at the connection between your mind and body by exploring the concept of the three brains within you: the head, heart, and gut. These three brains are crucial in helping you manage anxiety. By paying attention to the factors that influence your decision-making, you can make choices that align with your long-term goals, higher self, and the future you envision. When you listen to these three brains, you can ignore the messages that anxiety tries to impose on you and follow a path towards the reality you desire.

Before you can begin to process all of that, you need to understand the concept of the three brains your cognitive, emotional, and digestive intelligence. This is fascinating and supported by scientific evidence. The cognitive brain, located in the thinking part of your mind (*neocortex*), is responsible for processing information, making decisions, and engaging in logical thinking. The emotional brain, in the region of your mind that handles emotions (*limbic system*), influences your social interactions and how you bond with others, particularly in situations where certain behaviours are essential for survival. Finally, the gut brain, located in your gut (*enteric nervous system*), provides you with intuitive feelings, gut instincts, and the sensations associated with digestion.

Every day, your body's nervous system picks up on social cues around you, even without you realising it. These cues are processed by a part of your brain called grey matter, which helps with information processing and decision-making (Purves *et al.*, 2001). You can tap into your intuition by aligning your three brains—the head, heart, and gut—and make more accurate decisions. This connection between your brains also helps you manage anxiety, giving you control over your emotions and guiding your decision-making. Ultimately, it allows you to live a fulfilled and balanced life, free from anxiety and fear.

The concept of the three brains is based on human evolution. The gut brain, the oldest brain, helps us freeze in dangerous situations (see Chapter 7). The heart brain evolved next, allowing us to understand our own feelings and the emotions of others as social beings. The most recent and advanced thinking brain is responsible for logical thinking. It is located in the front part of your brain and is connected to a nerve called the *vagus nerve* (Porges, 1995). The vagus nerve, the longest cranial nerve in your body, regulates various bodily functions. It runs from your brainstem through your neck, chest, and abdomen, reaching different organs and body systems. The vagus nerve regulates heart rate, digestion, and other automatic bodily functions. It is also essential in facilitating communication between the brain and the body, carrying signals back and forth.

Each of the three brains processes different information and they constantly communicate with each other. Research shows that the heart and gut brain send more details to the head brain, influencing our decisions. By activating and optimising these three brains, we balance our nervous system, calming the mind and supporting the body.

These three brains (see Figure 4.1) affect our thoughts, emotions, and behaviours. When balanced, you can make effective decisions, regulate your emotions, and maintain overall well-being. However, an imbalance can lead to negative emotions like anxiety, stress, and depression. Understanding how these three brains function and interact can help us reduce the impact of pressure and create a more enjoyable life.

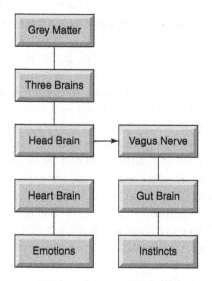

Figure 4.1 The Three-Brain Model

Figure 4.1 illustrates the relationship between grey matter and the three brains (head, heart, and gut). It also highlights the role of the vagus nerve in connecting the head brain with the heart and gut brain. The head brain is responsible for cognitive processing, while the heart brain processes emotions and the gut brain deals with instincts and intuition.

To illustrate the power of the three-brains equilibrium (3BE), let's look at a case example. One of my clients, let's call her Sarah, came to me with a common problem she was struggling with anxiety. She couldn't seem to move on from a difficult breakup. Sarah had been single for some time, and the thought of dating again triggered her worry even more especially in regard to her public eating habits.

Memories of her past relationship would surface, and negative thoughts about her gut health would consume her. However, Sarah was determined to take control of her negative emotions and find love again.

When we experience negative emotions such as stress, anxiety, or unhappiness, our brains can activate the release of *cortisol*. Cortisol is a hormone produced and released by the adrenal glands, located on top of the kidneys. Its primary role is to prepare the body for a response to potential threats or challenges. However, prolonged or frequent activation of cortisol due to negative emotions can have detrimental effects on our well-being. It can impact the immune system, raise blood pressure, and even contribute to weight gain. Therefore, it's important to manage stress and cultivate positive emotions to support overall health and well-being.

Sarah's journey to finding love was not an easy one. So together, we worked on those things that were in her control using the 3BE method, which is all about the power of intentional visualisation and positive thinking using encouraging self-talk, acting as if what you desire is already present and changing lifestyle habits. The impact of your thoughts on your emotions and hormones cannot be understated. When you engage in positive self-talk and visualisation, you can activate the release of *neurotransmitters* (chemical substances that transmit signals between nerve cells, or neurons, in the brain and other parts of the nervous system). *Serotonin* is a neurotransmitter that regulates mood, sleep, and appetite, contributing to feelings of well-being and happiness. *Dopamine* is a neurotransmitter associated with motivation, reward, and pleasure, influencing our motivation, goal-directed behaviour, and enjoyment of certain activities. Positive visualisation and affirmations can stimulate the production of serotonin and dopamine and other feel-good hormones like *oxytocin*, which helps you feel connected to others and fosters feelings of love and trust. This can improve your overall mood and increase your resilience to stress.

As Sarah's confidence grew with each session, using the 3BE method, she began to feel more empowered and began to trust her decisions. Her relationship with food improved as she convinced herself to try new foods with enthusiasm when she went out in public to eat in restaurants. Over time, the power of positive emotions like enthusiasm and joy fuelled her desire to find love.

Sarah made decisions that felt more aligned with her true self her instincts. This meant she didn't feel bad about what she was experiencing at the time of her decision-making. For instance, Sarah listened to the voice in her mind when she chose to experiment with different foods and eat in public places without the fear of being judged. She trusted herself to choose wisely and not turn to substitute drinks such as wine to suppress her nerves. Sarah's journey was not without challenges. Initially, she had doubts, anxiety, and fears about dating again, but her friend introduced her to someone special and she trusted her instincts. Sarah and her date hit it off, and they soon became best friends. They were in sync, not just with each other, but with themselves. Sarah's newfound balance between her mind, heart, and gut allowed her to find happiness.

You can draw inspiration from Sarah's journey and harness the innate power of your brain to shape a positive and fulfilling life for yourself through the practice of visualisation. By consciously directing your thoughts and focusing on positive outcomes, you have the ability to train your brain to release the feel-good chemicals that promote well-being. This involves examining situations logically, analysing how specific decisions make you feel, and humanising trust in the process. By embracing this approach, you can profoundly impact your overall well-being and create a life that is rich with positivity and fulfilment.

The Power of Visualisation

The process of intentional visualisation can be transformative. By intentionally envisioning the future of your dreams and focusing on positive outcomes, you can train your brains to release serotonin, dopamine, and create feelings of joy, enthusiasm, and fulfilment. This process allows you to connect with yourselves and others meaningfully, making a sense of purpose and happiness in your life. As you learn to tune into the messages from your heart and gut brains, you may find yourself making decisions that feel more aligned with your true self. This is because the heart and gut brains are thought to be more connected to your emotions and intuition than the head brain. By tapping into all three brains and allowing them to work together harmoniously, you can access a more holistic and integrated way of making choices. Research conducted by Soosal *et al.* (2019) has shown that this approach can lead to greater emotional regulation, improved decision-making, and better overall well-being. Sarah's story is an excellent example of how this can work in practice. Because she and I worked on her intention of gaining what she wanted at the beginning of the sessions, she could tap into her intuition and make decisions that felt right for her. This reduced her anxiety levels and gave her a sense of empowerment and control over her life.

Understanding the importance of cognitive intelligence and finding your niche is crucial for activating your brain's manifestation abilities. First, by focusing your intentions on growing your brain, you can enhance your cognitive abilities through continuous learning, mental exercises, physical activity, and maintaining a healthy lifestyle. Discovering your vocation enables you to channel your energy and efforts towards activities aligned with your passions and expertise. To effectively manifest improvement, it's essential to define your goals clearly, visualise success, use positive affirmations, and maintain consistency, while enhancing a positive mindset. By understanding your identity and purpose, you can unlock your brain's potential for manifestation.

Second, you can activate your emotional intelligence the feeling in your heart. This helps you manage your own moods more efficiently by anchoring genuine gratitude and appreciation for your life. When you let go of any expectations, anxiety, or memory of past adversity that may have held you back, you transform those feelings, switch the inner dialogue, and become confident to display your authentic self.

Third, and most important, is your digestive intelligence. This involves improving your nutrition according to your precise bodily needs, eating healthily, and improving digestion, which will make you feel more comfortable. Balancing that gut feeling is critical to good mental and emotional health.

Other ways to support brain activation include adopting breath-work practice, practising mindfulness and being present, and chanting a mantra out loud to stimulate the vagus nerve. Living a life of daily gratitude practice and genuinely appreciating life—because you live by practising mindfulness and only hold onto the good stuff—. This in turn activates your body's healing defences and affects each of your three brains.

Figure 4.2 represents the connection between positive self-talk, healthy eating, and the release of feel-good chemicals that promote well-being. At the centre of the diagram you have the three brains: the head (representing cognitive intelligence), the heart (representing emotional intelligence), and the gut (representing intuitive intelligence).

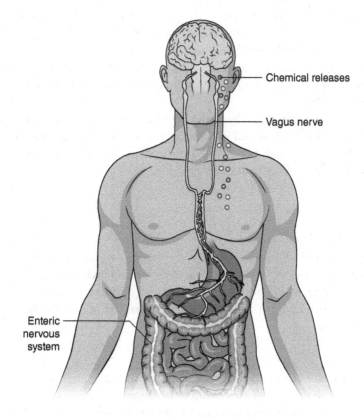

Figure 4.2 The Three Brain Pathways

From the head, positive self-talk and thoughts of making healthy choices send signals down the vagus nerve, which connects the brain to the heart and digestive system. These signals trigger a cascade of events. In the heart, the positive thoughts and self-talk stimulate the release of hormones such as dopamine and oxytocin, which promote feelings of joy, motivation, and connection. Simultaneously, the signals travel down to the gut, where they stimulate the enteric nervous system and the release of serotonin, another feel-good neurotransmitter. This promotes a sense of well-being and enhances digestive function. The heart and gut, in turn, send signals back up the vagus nerve to the brain, reinforcing the positive thoughts and self-talk and further amplifying the release of feel-good chemicals.

This interconnected loop of positive self-talk, healthy choices, and the release of feel-good chemicals creates a harmonious balance between the head, heart, and gut. It strengthens the connection and communication among the three brains, leading to improved overall well-being, emotional stability, and a sense of alignment with oneself.

Off course, the actual biological mechanisms are more complex. But by understanding and practising positive self-talk and making healthy choices, you can harness the power of these connections and promote a positive and fulfilling life.

3BE Methods

By activating and synchronising these three brains, you can create coherence and well-being in your life. Focusing on positive thoughts, practising gratitude, and improving nutrition and digestion can help you manifest what you desire. Listening to and harmonising your three brains leads to informed decision-making and a healthier, fearless self.

Having an Open Mind

It's crucial for you to first understand what resides in your head brain, which is associated with cognitive intelligence. This intelligence allows you to interpret meaning, form descriptions, and develop philosophies about yourself and the world around you. When you set aside emotions and employ logic and analysis to make decisions, you are utilising your head brain. Let me share an example to help you recognise how this can be applied.

Imagine a scenario where you are implementing a new project and need to select candidates for an internship. You find yourself in a dilemma because all the candidates are excellent, making it challenging to choose between them. To make a rational decision that benefits both you and the project, you need to approach the situation with reason and analysis. Consider the skills that each candidate would bring to the organisation. By engaging your head brain, you can narrow down the options and make a choice based on what is best for the company, rather than solely relying on emotions or gut feelings. By utilising internal language, understanding your feelings, considering intuitive choices, and thinking critically, your head brain supports you in making the right decision in this scenario.

Practising Empathy

Practising empathy involves tapping into the emotional intelligence housed in what we metaphorically refer to as the "heart brain". This area is associated with deep sensitivity and processes our feelings. It contains neurotransmitters, proteins, and support cells that contribute to our emotional experiences. The connection between the brain and the heart can be observed through the brain's ability to influence heart rate and the impact of increased stress on cardiovascular health.

If you consider yourself a highly empathetic person, it's important to remember that empathy is distinct from sympathy. I once had a client who believed that expensive cosmetic procedures would improve her self-worth. She had already undergone rhinoplasty but expressed concerns about affording therapy. During our discussions, I helped her realise that she had invested significant amounts of money in altering her appearance, hoping it would boost her self-worth. However, it hadn't resolved her underlying psychological issues, and she became even more critical of her perceived flaws. Through empathy, I mirrored her feelings back to her, helping her understand that investing less in changing her mindset would have a more profound impact on her happiness and self-perception. As she recognised her ability to control how she saw herself, her self-worth improved, and she made the decision to avoid further expensive cosmetic surgeries.

This instance underscores the pivotal role of the heart brain in decision-making and personal growth. It demonstrates how understanding and empathising with others' experiences can lead to transformative outcomes. By recognising the power of your emotions and values, you can make decisions that align with your true self and foster personal growth. The heart brain plays a crucial role in guiding us towards a more authentic life.

Trusting Your Intuition

Trusting your intuition and effectively utilising your three brains is crucial in navigating life's challenges. Your gut brain, also known as the enteric nervous system or digestive intelligence, plays a significant role in intuitive responses that may not be consciously realised. It comprehends situations before your head brain and can provide quick reactive responses based on instinct rather than reason.

This intuitive response is connected to the concept of "neuroception", a term coined by Steven Porges, which refers to the subconscious process of detecting cues of safety or threat in our environment (Porges, 2011). It is an automatic survival mechanism that operates through the autonomic nervous system, regulating bodily functions and stress responses. Neuroception, facilitated by the vagus nerve, allows us to evaluate the safety of our environment even before conscious perception of danger, triggering freeze or shutdown responses in the face of possible threats.

I often rely on my gut-brain instincts in challenging situations as a therapist. For instance, when dealing with a suicide incident on a bridge in London, I instinctively used my communication skills to connect with the person and talk about why they would want to jump off the bridge. My analytical and empathetic approach allowed me to articulate the right words, using my intuition about the situation. As a result, I was able to move the potential jumper to a safer position on the bridge, where the fire brigade and police could help them down. By tapping into the power of our gut brain, we can trust our instincts and make decisions that can help us and others in challenging situations.

The importance of using the 3BE method is that I'm prepared to act on my wisdom. If there is danger, I won't ignore my gut feelings. How often have you heard someone say that they ignored their gut instincts and deeply regretted it, triggering anxious feelings?

They say things like:

- "I knew something wasn't right."
- "I just had a sense I needed to speak to them."
- "I thought they were lying, but I just didn't trust myself enough."
- "It didn't look right somehow—but I went ahead anyway."

The gut brain can feel the most indirect to listen to. However, it is also one of the most crucial and instinctive ways your body connects to the world. The 3BE processes different kinds of data from your internal environment (the world inside your body) and your external environment (the world occurring outside your body). Because of this continuous communication, both your heart brain and gut brain are constantly surveying your environment and reporting back to the head brain and, most importantly, vice versa.

Remember in Chapter 2, when we reviewed the sympathetic nervous system that perceives a potential threat and prompts our body to respond, usually via an adrenaline rush that makes our bodies move away from danger. The second system is the parasympathetic system, which slows our heart rate, lowers blood pressure, and regulates digestion. When our bodies read a "not dangerous" cue, we calm down using the parasympathetic system.

When we activate our three brains through positive self-talk, set the intention, and visualise a calm, we can regulate our hormones and balance our whole nervous system by grounding ourselves in the present. So, it's essential to first come from a healthy and balanced baseline by calming the mind, nurturing the body, and gaining access to the three significant forms of intelligence by leading a healthy lifestyle.

Achieving equilibrium within the three brains involves several techniques that work in tandem to balance the head brain, heart brain, and gut brain.

Identifying equilibrium within yourself is a personal process that involves feeling, knowing, and utilising your body to ensure you're working towards balance. The equilibrium knows whether something makes sense to all three brains. Identifying a problem means there will be a solution, since every solution has a problem attached. When you decide, you sometimes feel a "click" and know you have reached the correct conclusion. If you don't get to that lightbulb moment, you may be ignoring input from one of your brains. Checking in regularly with yourself is vital, and you'll find that you already know all the answers just by how you feel.

Fix Me Tools

Practice Mindfulness. The head brain, where cognitive intelligence is stored, can be offset by practising mindfulness, yoga, brain gym, creativity, and stimulating concentration through puzzles, reading, playing games, and physical activity. By doing so, you will improve and balance your emotional and digestive intelligence, leading to overall well-being.

Connect With Your Emotions. The heart brain, where emotional intelligence is stored, is crucial in aligning your three brains. Connecting with your feelings by talking to others, instead of numbing or suppressing them, is an excellent way to strengthen this brain. Releasing emotions that keep you stuck and letting go of limiting beliefs by changing your perception of circumstances can also help you achieve equilibrium. Practising gratitude journalling, sitting with your pain, and transforming it are effective techniques to help you achieve emotional balance.

Manage Your Diet. The gut brain, where digestive intelligence is stored, is the most prominent sign of alignment. Digestion involves the intake that goes into our bodies, ultimately becoming the outcome. Digestive intelligence consists of holding onto or letting go of emotions, and being intuitive and mindful of your nutrition is key to achieving equilibrium. Eating a balanced and nutritious diet can help balance excesses and deficiencies through proper nutrition and nourishing your gut, ultimately strengthening your digestion. In addition, a healthy heart and stomach can increase immunity, ensuring optimal health.

In summary, when you activate your body's healing potential through practices like appreciating and being grateful for the good things in your life, taking care of yourself, spending time in nature, and maintaining a healthy lifestyle, you will have a profound impact on your three brains. By rewiring your head brain and positively influencing your heart brain, these practices create a state of balance and synchronisation throughout your body. This leads to improved well-being, increased satisfaction, and a happier, healthier, and more harmonious way of living.

Additionally, by cultivating a sense of balance and harmony within yourself, these practices can help you effectively manage anxiety, providing you with a powerful tool to find peace and resilience in the face of life's challenges. When you engage in positive self-talk and embrace these practices, you stimulate the release of chemicals in your brain that make you feel good, further supporting your well-being and emotional balance.

References

Porges, S. W. (1995). Orienting in a defensive world: Mammalian modifications of our evolutionary heritage. A polyvagal theory. *Psychophysiology*, 32(4), 301–318.

Porges, S. W. (2011). *The Polyvagal Theory: Neurophysiological Foundations of Emotions, Attachment, Communication, and Self-Regulation*. London: W. W. Norton & Co.

Purves, D., Augustine, G. J., Fitzpatrick, D., *et al.* (2001). *Neuroscience* (2nd ed.). Sunderland, MA: Sinauer Associates.

Soosal, P., Yawson, E. O., Asiedu-Addo, S. K. and Kang, H. Y. (2019). Three brains: Cephalic, cardiac and enteric. *African Journal of Neurological Sciences*, 38(1), 1–14.

5

Anxiety and Grief

....

As you continue your journey through this book, you will delve deeper into the root causes of anxiety and explore ways to manage your emotions. In the previous chapter, you learned the importance of aligning all three of your brains to use intuition and regulate the chemicals that impact your feelings. In this chapter, we will examine grief, a powerful emotion that can overwhelm you and make it difficult to control your feelings.

Navigating grief can be a challenging experience. It's important to understand that grief is a complex emotion that can leave you feeling lost and broken. As you continue your journey through this book, we will now explore strategies to help you manage grief and other intense emotions. By utilising the tools and techniques you have learned, you can gradually regain control over your emotions and find healing and acceptance.

Grief is not solely limited to the loss of a loved one. It can be triggered by various other losses, such as the loss of financial stability, a home, or a sense of identity. Each person's experience of grief is unique, and it's crucial to recognise and respect that. While grief can feel overwhelming, there are ways to manage the intense emotions associated with it. By acknowledging the normalcy of the grieving process and allowing yourself to feel the emotions that arise, you can gradually find meaning and healing in the aftermath of grief.

Grief and anxiety often go hand in hand, as the unknown and the loss of emotional security can intensify both emotions. However, by actively engaging in the grieving process and utilising available resources, you can emerge from grief with a renewed sense of purpose and resilience.

The grieving process refers to the natural and individual journey one goes through after experiencing a significant loss, such as the death of a loved one, the end of a relationship, or the loss of a job. While everyone's experience of grief is unique, there are commonly recognised stages or phases that many people may go through.

In her book, psychiatrist, Elisabeth Kübler-Ross talks about The five stages of grief, commonly known as the Kübler-Ross model, (Kübler-Ross, 2008).

The stages, which describe the emotional and psychological responses individuals may experience when facing their own mortality, or the loss of a loved one, are as follows. These stages are not necessarily sequential and can overlap or occur in different orders. It's important to note that not everyone will experience all the stages, and the intensity and duration of each stage can vary.

- **Denial.** Initially, individuals may experience a sense of disbelief or denial, avoiding the reality of the loss. This can serve as a protective mechanism, allowing them to gradually come to terms with the loss at their own pace.
- **Anger.** As the reality of the loss sets in, individuals may feel anger, frustration, or resentment. They may direct their anger towards themselves, others, or even the person who has passed away.
- **Bargaining.** This stage involves seeking ways to regain what was lost or trying to make sense of the situation. People may find themselves making promises or attempting to negotiate with a higher power, hoping to undo the loss.
- **Depression.** Feelings of sadness, emptiness, and a deep sense of loss are common during this stage. It's important to differentiate

between grief-related depression, which is a natural response to loss, and clinical depression, which may require professional intervention.

- **Acceptance.** This stage is characterised by coming to terms with the reality of the loss. It doesn't mean that the pain completely disappears, but individuals begin to find a way to live with the loss and adjust to the new normal.

It's important to remember that the grieving process is not a linear path, and individuals may move back and forth between these stages. Additionally, not everyone will experience all these stages, and some individuals may find their own unique ways of coping with grief. Each person's journey through grief is highly personal and influenced by various factors, such as cultural background, support system, and individual coping mechanisms.

Reflecting on my recent experience with grief after the loss of my beloved pet dog, Chico, in July 2023, I have encountered moments of denial, confusion, and guilt. We will look at pet grief in the next chapter. It took time for me to fully comprehend the depth of my emotions during this difficult period. Guilt, in particular, is a profound aspect of the grieving process that I often encounter with my clients. It can arise for various reasons. Firstly, individuals may feel a sense of responsibility for the loss, believing they could have prevented it or acted differently. Secondly, survivor guilt may manifest, causing them to feel guilty for being alive while their loved one is not. Lastly, unresolved conflicts or regrets with the deceased can intensify feelings of guilt and complicate the grieving journey. In my own situation, I questioned whether I could have responded to my dog's needs more effectively. Recognising the significance of guilt in the emotional and psychological stages of grief, I believe it is crucial to address and navigate these feelings compassionately and seek support during the healing process.

As mentioned, the journey through grief is not linear, and it's normal to experience a range of emotions such as numbness, sadness, anger, and even intense anxiety. However, by recognising and acknowledging these emotions, seeking support, and engaging in self-care practices, you can navigate the grieving process and discover inner strength and resilience.

Generational Patterns

I know that it is easier said than done. But if you have someone to help you understand the process and break the cycle of how you manage grief, the management of the emotions, particularly the anxiety, will become easier to process. Initially, when I experienced significant losses, such as the death of my father and my beloved dog, Lucky, from childhood, I didn't have the emotional tools to process those losses. As a child, I witnessed my mother struggling with anxiety and emotional regulation, which had become repetitive. These are known as *transgenerational* patterns and can be positive or negative. I learned to cope with my emotions by repressing them and turning to anxiety. Unfortunately, this anxiety and emotional repression pattern continued into adulthood, and I experienced more losses, including losing my childhood home, friends, dreams, and love. I felt like I was losing everything, and the pattern kept repeating even after marriage, loss of motherhood, divorce, financial loss and, again, my home. Nevertheless, I held onto the grief.

Grief can be overwhelming, consuming, and compound over time, especially if experienced but not expressed. This was the case for me. The repressed grief around my father's death and other events resulted in a layer cake of emotions I had not dealt with. So, when three of my school friends died in a road accident, it hit my other school friends and me even harder.

I developed a close relationship with a woman whom I call "Aunty", a common and respectful title in my Indian culture. Tragically, she lost her youngest child, Sukhi, in the same accident that took the lives of my school friends. As I got to know her, I noticed a similar transgenerational loss and emotional repression pattern in her life. Her husband had also left her, taking their eldest child with him, leaving her with a deep sense of rejection. She inherited a pattern of emotional repression and felt the need to conform to societal expectations, compounding her grief and anxiety. She was engulfed in these emotions and still suffers from chronic depression due to bereavement today, struggling to process her loss and move forward. It is a heart-breaking reminder that transgenerational patterns can significantly impact our emotional well-being and healing process.

I've realised that patterns of behaviour, belief, and emotion can be inherited and passed down from one generation to the next within a family. For example, patterns can repeat themselves even when we believe death is out of control. I saw this first-hand in my family when my father's youngest brother, my Uncle Pomma, died at precisely the same age as my father from a head injury. It's hard not to see this as a transgenerational pattern, especially considering other similarities between their lives. This realisation has made me more aware of the potential impact of transgenerational patterns in my life and has encouraged me to be more intentional about breaking any negative habits I may have inherited.

For instance, a family may have a tradition of kindness or a shared love of music, which are positive transgenerational patterns. On the other hand, some families may have patterns of abuse or addiction, which are negative transgenerational patterns. In my case, the transgenerational pattern was negative and manifested as a pattern of anxiety and emotional repression. However, it is possible to break these patterns and move forward with self-awareness and healthy coping mechanisms. By understanding the different types of grief and how they affect us, we can start to recognise our emotions and work towards healing. I know grief is a complex emotion that can take many forms, affecting everyone differently. Expressing grief through healthy channels like therapy, support groups, or simply talking to a trusted friend can be a significant step in recovery.

Experiencing grief can be overwhelming and consuming, leading to feeling stuck and unable to move on. Many fear that letting go of suffering will mean forgetting the person or pet they lost, leading to a sense of guilt or betrayal. This can be particularly true for those who have lost a child, as the situation seems unfair and unjust. When explaining this to the family members of my clients, I often find that they struggle to understand why their loved ones need to hold onto their grief. However, it's essential to recognise that letting go of the past doesn't mean forgetting it. It means coping with the loss and moving forward while honouring the memories of the loved one's life. The anxiety from holding onto grief is a side-effect of unexpressed or unmanaged emotions, and the pain can be immense. I've experienced this and know how difficult it can be to confront and process these emotions. Dwelling on what could have been, or what should have been, is not helpful in the therapeutic process. Instead, we must learn to cope with our grief and find healthy ways to move forward while still honouring the memories of our loved ones.

Losing someone close, such as a family member or a dear friend, is one of the most challenging experiences anyone can face in life. The pain of grief is unique and profound, and it can last a lifetime, as it sadly has for Aunty. Even for those who can find ways to live with their grief, the loss remains a part of them, shaping the person they become. As I've learned through my own experiences and those of others, there is no set timetable for grieving, no standard to which we should hold ourselves. It's not a matter of "getting over it" or moving on, because the pain of loss never truly disappears. We can learn to live with our grief and get through it, but we must also acknowledge that the experience is unique to each individual, and we all cope in our own way. Whether we find solace in religion, therapy, support groups, or simply the passage of time, we must never compare ourselves to others or feel pressure to meet a certain standard. Grief is a complicated process, and giving ourselves the time and space to heal is important.

How to Settle Your Grief

Grieving can lead to intense anxiety, and knowing and understanding such emotions is crucial for settling into your life with that pain. Anxiety can manifest as a compounding layer of pain from your past that can be overwhelming and debilitating. Recognising and comprehending how you process your emotions can help you navigate the anxiety that comes with grief. This section offers additional thoughts on what you can do to cope with anxiety and despair.

I experienced profound grief during my miscarriages and divorce. The end of my marriage was excruciating, as it felt like my ex-husband took away my chance at motherhood. The emotional toll was compounded by a life-threatening surgery after my final miscarriage, when I lost my twins. Feeling unsupported by my ex-husband's family, especially, added to my grief. Despite these difficult circumstances, I learned valuable lessons through my journey with grief.

The loss of my dreams and the possibility of motherhood brought intense pain and physical manifestations. My heart ached, my body weakened, and I experienced symptoms like difficulty breathing, dizziness, and headaches. Loneliness and isolation deepened, making even simple tasks overwhelming and exhausting.

So how can we settle such pain? Through self-therapy and self-care practices, I found ways to manage the symptoms of grief and start rebuilding my life. Although the pain still exists, even more so now that I have lost my companion, Chico. I learned to integrate it into my life in a way that allowed me to move forward with grace and understanding. This drive to thrive worked for me. I discovered so many talents hidden within me. I liked hiking and painting, and my writing for purpose to support and entertain people became my baby. The lesson of my past has taught me that it's possible to find a way to live with the pain and move forward, building a new future for yourself.

Despite the difficulty of the circumstances, I am grateful for the lessons I learned, I certainly would not be where I am today in my career if they were not a part of my fate. Living with grief is an overwhelming and challenging journey. It can leave us feeling lost and unable to move forward. Personally, this was especially true after my divorce, when I had to leave behind everything that was familiar to me. Despite the uncertainty at that time, I found solace in the company of my beloved Newfoundland dog, Chico, as we faced the future together.

I was grateful for the offer of a place to stay at my brother's home, even if it was just a quilt on my mother's bedroom floor during his house renovations. However, this kind gesture did little to ease the weight of my emotions. The uncertainty added to my anxiety and compounded my grief, leaving me feeling stuck and lost.

Through my grief journey, I've learned to challenge societal expectations and timelines that can be superficial and unhelpful. It's crucial to recognise that your suffering is unique, and it's important to honour and process it authentically, taking the time you need to grieve.

One valuable lesson I've learned is to be patient with myself. As I keep repeating, grieving is deeply personal, and there's no right or wrong way to navigate it. Pressuring yourself to overcome grief or adhere to a specific timeline only intensifies the pain. It's okay to feel lost and uncertain, allowing yourself the space to not have all the answers. By embracing your grief on your own terms, you will gain clarity and a deeper understanding of yourself.

Settling grief is complex, but it begins with recognising your worth. Accepting the reality of the situation and allowing yourself to feel sadness is crucial for moving forward. Self-care should not be neglected, as it can prevent a spiral of sorrow that leaves you feeling stuck, isolated, and alone.

Fix Me Tools

Overcome Guilt and Allow Others to Help. It's crucial to overcome guilt about asking for help. Everyone copes differently, and it's your pain, your journey. So please don't feel bad about asking for help when needed.

Talk to a Professional. Talking to a professional about your grief can help you process and understand your emotions better. For example, a doctor can put you in touch with a professional bereavement counsellor, or you can find one on your own.

Avoid Medication. It's sometimes easy to turn to medications to get through grief. This may add to the anxiety, especially on challenging days, but it's best to avoid taking medicines unless prescribed by your doctor.

Maintain Routine and Eat Healthily. If household members share your grief, keep a routine as much as possible, especially if young children are involved. Eating and drinking healthily can help maintain sleep, and emotional and mental stability.

Be Prepared for Occasions. Be prepared for occasions triggering anxiety or the sudden onset of tears, such as birthdays, anniversaries, and events. If this happens, practise some of the exercises shared earlier in the book to control the pain.

In this chapter I have explained the profound and complex experience of loss, shedding light on the challenges and emotions that accompany significant life events. I delved into the impact of transgenerational patterns on our emotional well-being, emphasising the importance of breaking negative patterns and finding healthy coping mechanisms. Through personal narratives and insights, this chapter guides you in settling your grief by acknowledging its unique nature, practising self-care, and seeking support. It encourages you to accept the pain, understanding that healing doesn't mean forgetting, and to find ways to honour the past while moving forward with clarity and self-awareness. It is important to remember that we all have our own personal experiences, and there is no clear division between one step and the next. However, as time passes, the intensity of anxiety diminishes, and healing becomes possible. Remember to establish a framework for managing emotions and be patient with yourself. Reach out to friends, loved ones, or professionals who genuinely care about your well-being. Your journey to living with grief is distinctive to you, and it begins with your own actions and choices.

Reference

Kübler-Ross, E. (2008). *On Death and Dying*. London: Simon & Schuster.

6

Pet and Pet Owners' Anxiety

....

I would like to dedicate this chapter to my beloved dog, Chico (August 2011–July 2023). Building upon the valuable lessons you learned in Chapter 5 on grief, we now shift our focus to a related but distinct topic: pet and pet owners' anxiety. Although this book primarily focuses on human experiences, it's essential to acknowledge that our pets also experience anxiety, and this can affect your well-being too. If you don't own a pet, you may choose to skip this chapter. But if you're a pet owner or interested in understanding pet behaviour and your reaction to it, you will benefit from delving into the different types of pet and pet owners' anxiety.

While the previous chapter explored the complexities of human grief, it's important to recognise that our pets also experience anxiety, profoundly impacting their well-being and yours. In this chapter, we will explore the different forms of pet anxiety, such as separation anxiety and grief-related anxiety, and offer practical strategies to help you navigate these complex emotions. By understanding and addressing pet anxiety, you can support a stronger bond with your animal companion and promote your own emotional well-being.

I like to believe that if you have a pet, it brings you tremendous joy and fulfilment, but as I used to be a pet owner myself, I know that it also comes with a sense of responsibility and anxiety, especially if you're a first-time pet owner. When your pet has behavioural issues or health concerns, this can cause stress and worry, leading to pet anxiety in both you and your companion. Separation anxiety is another common type of pet anxiety that occurs when your pet becomes anxious and agitated when you're away; or you may experience anxiety when leaving your pet under the care of another person. The grief of losing a pet can also be overwhelming, impacting your daily life. In the following sections I will briefly explore each type of pet anxiety, and at the end of the chapter provide practical strategies to help you navigate these complex emotions. By understanding the different types of pet anxiety and developing strategies to address them, you can build a stronger bond with your pet and better understand why anxiety presents itself if you are responsible for a pet.

If you're a pet owner, you may connect deeply with your animal companions, treating them like family. However, as your pet ages, you may become anxious and worried about their well-being, leading to stress and concern. This anxiety can heighten when others comment on your pet's age or health, triggering a sense of fear for their safety. I know this all too well. I had a very special bond with my dog, Chico, who as a puppy saved my life by pulling me out of an unconscious state after a miscarriage. As Chico grew older, I noticed increased anxiety about his health and happiness, causing me to worry about his well-being. It's natural for us as pet owners to feel this way, but finding healthy ways to manage these emotions is essential to ensure your pet receives the best care possible.

Separation Anxiety

As a therapist, I have had numerous conversations with pet owners who experience anxiety when leaving their pets behind. It's not just pets that feel anxious; humans can also feel a sense of worry and fear for their pet's safety and well-being. This anxiety can be triggered by fear of the unknown and concern about their pet's loneliness. Moreover, pets are highly attuned to their owner's emotions, which can create a cycle of anxiety and guilt for both pet and owner.

One of my clients, Greg, exemplifies this anxiety. He is highly anxious about leaving his pet alone and expresses deep guilt and fear regarding his dog's well-being. This type of anxiety is known as separation anxiety, a common form of pet anxiety. Research has shown that dogs with separation anxiety are more likely to exhibit other stress-related behaviours, such as noise sensitivity and fear of unfamiliar people or objects. Recognising the significance of addressing separation anxiety, I have worked closely with Greg and other clients to find effective strategies. I know it's not easy to recognise human behaviour at times, let alone animal behaviour. Nevertheless, I thought it an important topic to cover, considering that more than a third of the world's population are pet owners.

One approach I recommended to Greg is establishing a routine for his pet. Regular feeding, exercise, and playtime provide pets with stability and security, helping reduce anxiety and stress. Interactive toys and games can also keep pets occupied and entertained while their owners are away. Additionally, seeking support from friends, family, or even a therapist is crucial. Pet owners must understand that pet-related anxiety is common, and reaching out for assistance is acceptable. Self-therapy, or any type of talk therapy, can provide coping techniques and a safe space to address concerns and worries. Gradually exposing the pet to short periods of separation is another helpful strategy. The pet can become more comfortable and confident in being alone by starting with brief periods and progressively increasing the time. This approach helps reduce anxiety and build familiarity with separation. It gives you, as a pet owner, a sense of forming a structure that is to the benefit of both yourself and your pet.

Leaving pets in the care of others can also cause anxiety in both humans and their animal companions. I recommend finding a trusted and reliable pet sitter or boarding facility with positive reviews and references to alleviate this concern. Provide detailed instructions about the pet's routine, diet, and medication or health concerns. Regular check-ins and updates from the pet sitter or boarding facility can provide peace of mind and reduce separation anxiety. Additionally, staying in touch through video calls or messages can help maintain a sense of connection and comfort.

Another client, Jen, experienced overwhelming guilt and stress as a new pet owner. She felt she was not providing everything her pet needed, and this guilt impacted her overall well-being. I reminded Jen that it's essential to acknowledge that guilt is a common emotion reported by pet owners, often stemming from the belief that they are not adequately meeting their pet's needs. Understanding that mistakes happen and seeking support from reliable resources—such as books, scientific studies, and experienced pet owners can provide invaluable guidance and reassurance.

I advised Greg and Jen to join a community or group of pet owners. This can offer tremendous support and a platform to share experiences and tips on caring for a new pet. Establishing a daily routine incorporating proper care, feeding, and exercise helps create stability and security for pet and owner. Seeking assistance from animal behaviourists or trainers can address potential behavioural issues and develop a healthy relationship between owner and pet. Animals pick up on senses. They know when the chemical, cortisol, releases in their owners and this in turn makes them seem more agitated.

When I explained this to Jen, who found her new pet owner journey extremely challenging, she began to make small changes. She established a routine and addressed her guilt through therapy; she began to appreciate the benefits of pet ownership. Over time, she grew more confident in caring for her pet, and their bond strengthened. This highlights the positive impact that pet ownership can have on mental health, with studies showing lower levels of depression and anxiety among pet owners compared to non-pet owners (Brooks *et al.*, 2016).

Remember that being a pet owner is a learning process, and making mistakes is normal. Seeking support, establishing routines, and providing the best care possible promotes the well-being of both pet and owner. The rewards of pet ownership including companionship, comfort, and joy are immeasurable, and enrich the lives of people from all walks of life.

As a therapist I understand the natural fears and anxieties of being a pet owner. Over time, as you settle into a routine, that initial anxiety tends to ease. However, as your beloved pet ages and you observe signs of their physical decline, that anxiety can resurface. The fear of losing your faithful companion can be overwhelming, and it's a feeling shared by countless pet owners worldwide. The secret to this is to remain calm and enjoy the moments you have with your pet. When pets are in the presence of a peaceful and relaxed owner, their bodies can release oxytocin, commonly known as the "love hormone". Oxytocin is a chemical released into your body that plays a role in social bonding, trust, and positive emotions. It is associated with feelings of love, affection, and relaxation. When a pet senses its owner's calm state, this can trigger the release of oxytocin in both pet and owner, promoting a sense of well-being and strengthening the bond between them.

Grief-Related Anxiety: Loss of a Pet

Sadly, I lost my companion of nearly 12 years, and I won't lie, no matter how prepared you may think that you are losing a faithful companion who gives unconditional love can be devastating. Grief and pet owner anxiety are sensitive topics that researchers and mental health professionals agree deserve more attention. While statistics vary from country to country, as mentioned, over a third of the world's population are pet owners highlighting the significance of this issue. The tie between a pet and its owner can be incredibly strong, and when that connection is severed by death, the resulting grief can be overwhelming. Losing Chico has left me feeling broken, and my heart aches even today.

Guilt can compound the grief experienced when losing a pet, especially if the difficult decision to euthanise them was made. Despite Chico passing away peacefully in the presence of his immediate family, I couldn't help but feel an overwhelming sense of guilt, questioning if I had missed signs of his discomfort or failed to provide him with enough love. Knowing that Chico died of old age didn't ease my pain. This guilt and anxiety can create a relentless cycle of rumination, causing further doubt about the decision made and intensifying the grief and anxiety. It's important to recognise these feelings as a normal part of the grieving process and to practice self-compassion, seeking support from loved ones or professionals specialising in pet bereavement. Remembering the love and care given to Chico throughout his life has allowed me to grieve, while being gentle and understanding to myself about how he didn't suffer has helped me through the healing process.

If you feel responsible for a pet's well-being, you must recognise that these feelings are valid and seek support. The grieving process takes time, and giving yourself the space and grace to heal is essential. In addition, remembering the joy and companionship that your pet brought into your life can help ease the pain of their loss and honour their memory.

The experience of losing a pet can have a profound and enduring emotional impact on both the pet owner and those close to them. This became evident when I shared my grief over losing Chico with my cousin, who had previously faced the difficult decision of euthanising her beloved dog, Cody. As she spoke about her own grief, it triggered a flood of memories and emotions related to the loss of my childhood dog, Lucky. The intensity of these emotions, coupled with palpitations and anxiety, reminded me of the deep sorrow that pet loss can bring, even after years have passed. This emphasises the immense significance of pet loss and its potential to profoundly affect our mental well-being.

It's essential to recognise the intensity of emotions associated with pet loss, practice self-care, and seek support from loved ones, friends, or a therapist to navigate the grieving process constructively. Honouring our pet's memory can help us find a sense of peace and acceptance amidst the loss. By acknowledging the validity of our emotions and seeking support, we can begin to manage our anxiety and move forward positively. Remember, it's natural to feel the pain of losing a pet, and seeking help is a sign of strength and self-care.

The loss of a pet can have a profound emotional impact, triggering intense feelings of sadness, guilt, loneliness, and anxiety. The bond between a pet and its owner is often deep, and when that bond is broken, it can leave an emotional wound that takes a long time to heal. Anxiety symptoms such as sweating, a racing heart, trembling, and difficulty breathing can be common responses to the stress and trauma associated with pet loss. Anticipatory anxiety the fear of losing a beloved pet can also be a significant source of stress, which can interfere with daily activities. Furthermore, the lack of understanding and support around pet loss can exacerbate anxiety, leaving those grieving without the necessary support systems to cope with their emotions. Disenfranchised grief and the absence of established social rituals around losing a pet can make it challenging to process grief, leading to isolation and anxiety. Additionally, invalidating comments that fail to acknowledge the depth of the connection between a pet and its owner can trigger anxiety, making the grieving process even more challenging. Recognising and acknowledging the intensity of emotions associated with pet loss, including anxiety, is essential for those who experience it. Seeking support can help you manage stress and move through the grieving process. By honouring your pet's memory, finding healthy ways to cope with your grief, you can navigate the grieving process and emerge stronger.

As we have learned, heartbreak due to the loss of a pet can be an intense and overwhelming experience, which can trigger anxiety-related disorders. Recognising and acknowledging the intensity of the associated emotions including anxiety, sadness, guilt, and fear is essential. Past trauma or experiences can also exacerbate anxiety-related disorders after pet loss. Therefore, finding ways to pay tribute to your pet and remember your pet can help manage the anxiety and pain associated with pet bereavement.

While pet loss is a deeply personal journey that takes time and patience, some coping mechanisms and techniques can help ease the pain and anxiety. Talking to someone about your feelings can provide a supportive and validating environment for processing grief. Engaging in activities that bring comfort and joy such as exercise, art, or time in nature can also help ease anxiety and promote healing. Finding ways to honour and remember the pet, such as creating a memorial or performing a meaningful ritual, can provide a sense of closure and comfort. These are all the things that are helping me. As soon as Chico passed, I shared my relationship with Chico on my social media platforms. I found that people shared the same sorrow, where they had also lost a pet. I am grateful that Chico went so peacefully; his kind and loving vet, Jose, made sure that Chico was comfortable. And as a family we honoured Chico's departure the next day at a pet crematorium, where everyone close to Chico attended. I now have a ring with his ashes and a little area in my home to memorialise Chico, and although my heart hurts, doing these things helps. I also talk to my friends and family who have lost pets. I'll repeat it: Remember, the pain of pet loss is valid, and seeking help and support is a sign of strength and self-care.

One of the most significant things you can do is fully mourn the loss of your pet. Allow yourself to feel all the emotions of the grieving process, including sadness, guilt, anger, and denial. When situational anxiety becomes too much to bear and affects your ability to work, eat, sleep, or concentrate, it is important to communicate those feelings. Talking to loved ones, friends, or neighbours, or even chatting online with people who have had a similar experience, can help.

It is common to feel guilty, or like you must justify the time taken to grieve your pet's loss. However, it is essential to remember that you do not have to feel guilty about taking the time you need to get through the grief. Losing a pet can be just as distressing as losing any other important figure in your life, and as I said in Chapter 5, there is no right or wrong way to grieve.

Learning to accept and sit with the feelings and emotions you are experiencing is also crucial. When you understand your emotions, you are better able to understand your thoughts, and these thoughts can help you maintain the anxiety and reason with your feelings. The key here is to know why you are experiencing the emotions or specific symptoms, such as changes in mood or sensations of hurt.

Fix Me Tools

Join a Support Group. Consider joining a pet loss support group where you can share your feelings and experiences with others who have also lost a pet. This can help you feel less alone and make a safe space available to talk about your emotions.

Seek Professional Help. If you are struggling to cope with your grief, consider seeking professional help from a therapist or counsellor specialising in pet loss. They can help you work through your emotions and provide you with coping strategies to manage your anxiety.

Engage in Self-Care. Make sure you care for yourself physically, emotionally, and mentally. This includes eating well, exercising, getting enough sleep, and taking time for yourself to relax and unwind.

Memorialise Your Pet. Creating a memorial for your pet can be a therapeutic way to honour their memory and provide a sense of closure. Consider creating a photo album or frame, planting a tree in their memory, or creating a particular piece of art. Like I shared earlier, I had a piece of jewellery made from some of Chico's ashes.

Practise Gratitude. Focus on the positive memories you shared with your pet and express gratitude for your time together. Practising gratitude can help shift your focus away from your anxiety and towards the positive aspects of your relationship with your pet.

Write About Your Feelings. Keeping a journal or writing about your feelings can help you process your emotions and work through your grief. For example, write about your favourite memories with your pet, your feelings, and any thoughts or emotions that arise.

Connect With Nature. Time in nature can be a healing experience and help you feel more grounded. Take a walk in the park, hike, or spend time gardening to connect with the natural world.

Be a Volunteer. Consider volunteering at an animal shelter or rescue organisation in memory of your pet. This can be a meaningful way to honour their memory and give back to other needy animals.

Anxiety after pet loss is a normal reaction to the grief you are experiencing. Acknowledging and processing your emotions and caring for yourself during this difficult time is essential. Use the coping strategies shared in this chapter and remember to be patient and compassionate with yourself as you work through your grief. Remember, the love you shared with your pet will always be with you, even though they are no longer physically present.

Reference

Brooks, H., Rushton, K., Walker, S., Lovell, K. and Rogers, A. (2016). Ontological security and connectivity provided by pets: A study in the self-management of the everyday lives of people diagnosed with a long-term mental health condition. *BMC Psychiatry*, 16(1). DOI: 10.1186/s12888-018-1613-2.

7

Fear and the Fight, Flight, Freeze, and Fawn Responses

···

Reflecting on the preceding chapter, I was struck by the emotional responses of pet owners dealing with losing their beloved companions. Fear is a primal instinct triggered by various factors, including uncertainty, the fear of losing someone or something, and the fear of the future. This chapter will explore fear and its physiological and psychological responses. Here I want to examine the fight–flight–freeze and fawn response, an innate coping mechanism that prepares humans to adapt to stress using the sympathetic branch of the autonomic nervous system. However, excessive or inappropriate triggering of this response can lead to physical and emotional symptoms associated with anxiety.

Traumatic events can trigger a physiological response in the body, releasing hormones that regulate various processes and maintain balance. These hormonal imbalances can profoundly impact our survival systems, such as control, connection, and meaning in life.

Moreover, research highlights the vital link between past trauma and the development of anxiety disorders, particularly in childhood. How adults model and respond to fear plays a crucial role in shaping children's fear responses, as children learn from observing adult behaviour. By demonstrating healthy coping strategies and fostering a supportive environment, adults can positively influence children's fear responses and help them develop resilience in the face of anxiety.

I am from an Indian culture, brought up to fear what others would think of me and the reputation of my family if I did not study. Judgement and high performance were a huge anxiety trigger for me. As I learned later in life, I did what I was told as a child to please my parents, relatives, and community, and achieve a sense of belonging. In reality, my biggest fear had always been rejection. If I did not live up to the expectations, I would not belong.

In his book, therapist and researcher Pete Walker explores the impact of repetitive childhood trauma on your survival responses. For example, Walker discusses the fight–flight–freeze and fawn responses, where you may feel strongly inclined to please others to avoid harm or rejection (Walker, 2013). These responses are deeply rooted in your primitive defence mechanisms and can have both adaptive and maladaptive effects, depending on the situation. Understanding these survival responses can help you navigate the impact of childhood trauma and develop healthier coping strategies for emotional regulation and resilience. By recognising these patterns and working towards a more balanced and resilient state, you can fully expand your capacity to experience and embrace life.

Understanding Resilience

Resilience is the ability to adapt, bounce back, and thrive in the face of adversity, setbacks, or challenging circumstances, demonstrating emotional strength, flexibility, and a positive mindset. It is the key to effectively managing fear and anxiety in response to stressful situations. Understanding the various reactions to fear, such as the fight–flight–freeze and fawn responses, and acknowledging the role of trauma, empowers us to develop more effective strategies for handling fear and anxiety. In addition, building resilience involves seeking support from caring individuals in our lives, including peers, partners, and colleagues, while fostering open dialogue and mutual understanding. Studies have shed light on the immobilisation or submissiveness response, which can be triggered by severe trauma or intense fear. Conversely, the fawn response is characterised by an inclination to please or appease perceived threats. By delving into the complexity of human fear responses, we gain valuable insights into our emotional experiences and learn how to support people who are struggling. Furthermore, understanding these responses is crucial for comprehending the formation of specific phobias, as traumatic experiences shape our reactions and can trigger specific fears or anxieties.

Reflecting on personal experiences, there are memorable instances when individuals have faced fear head-on and demonstrated non-fear-based responses. For example, my grandmother's calm and composed demeanour during a precarious situation, when she saved my life from falling from a cliff, taught me valuable lessons on managing fear in healthier ways. This chapter aims to build upon such insights, comprehensively understanding fear, its different responses, and effective coping strategies. By exploring and comprehending our reactions to fear, we can effectively develop valuable tools to manage fear and anxiety.

Numerous researchers have conducted studies on the fight–flight–freeze response, with Walter Cannon being one of the earliest pioneers in investigating physiological responses to stress (Cannon, 1915). Cannon identified the fight–flight response as a critical survival mechanism. Another significant contributor to our understanding of the physiological stress response is W. Bradford, whose work laid the foundation for the concept of the autonomic nervous system (Bradford, 1920).

While research on the immobilisation or submissiveness response is still in its early stages, studies have shown that individuals who have experienced trauma may be more susceptible to developing anxiety disorders due to the lasting impact of trauma on their body's stress response. To overcome these patterns, I encourage individuals to develop self-awareness of their body and its sensations, utilise techniques outlined in this book to regulate and calm the nervous system through positive self-talk, and establish healthy boundaries that prioritise self-care.

Understanding the different forms of the fight–flight–freeze and fawn response is crucial in effectively managing fear and anxiety. By becoming more attuned to our emotional and physical reactions to fear, we can cultivate resilience and cope with fear and anxiety in healthy and constructive ways. This may involve challenging negative thoughts and beliefs, seeking support from others, or practising relaxation techniques. By mastering our fear response, we can lead more fulfilling and productive lives unencumbered by the limitations of fear and anxiety.

Managing Fear: The Underlying Root

A study by Lazarus and Folkman (1984) found that how individuals perceive and cope with a situation determines their level of fear. In other words, fear is not just a result of the problem itself, but also of how you perceive it and your ability to cope with it. This study highlights the importance of reframing your mindset and beliefs to better cope with fear and anxiety-provoking situations.

Fear can significantly impact an individual's life, as demonstrated by a lady I met on a flight. Sara sat beside me on a flight from New York to Florida. Before the flight had taken off, Sara had shared that she had a fear of flying after encountering turbulence on a previous flight, and she was anxious about this flight. Sara's fear was palpable, and she confided that she needed to fly due to a sick relative, which worsened her anxiety. Fear can be so ingrained that even the mere thought of flying can trigger anxiety and physical symptoms, such as increased sweating and a raised heart rate. It can also restrict an individual's ability to travel for work or pleasure, limiting experiences and causing distress.

As a therapist, once I gained a rapport with Sara, I offered to help her overcome her fear—but due to time constraints, I had to use hypnosis to help her cope. I induced a hypnotic state in Sara and provided her with visualisation and relaxation techniques to access her subconscious mind and achieve a state of deep relaxation and focus. In the hypnotic state, I asked Sara to visualise herself on the plane, feeling safe and secure. I encouraged her to picture the pilot and crew, trained professionals capable of handling any situation. I also asked her to imagine the plane taking off smoothly and soaring through the clouds effortlessly, surrounded by other passengers who were relaxed and enjoying their flight.

Through these visualisations, Sara felt a sense of calm and relaxation, realising that she was safe and secure. She also learned to control her thoughts and emotions, which allowed her to let go of any fear or anxiety she was experiencing. With the help of positive affirmations, she reinforced her sense of safety and security, focusing on breathing and anchoring herself in the present moment.

Sara used this visualisation and relaxation technique during the rest of the flight, reducing her anxiety and regaining control of her fear. While hypnosis may not work for everyone, it demonstrates how effective techniques—such as exposure therapy and cognitive-behavioural therapy—can manage fear and anxiety. Additionally, self-hypnosis can be used as a powerful technique for individuals to induce a hypnotic state in themselves without needing a therapist or external induction. Through self-suggestion and relaxation techniques, individuals can access their subconscious mind and plant positive affirmations or visualisations, enabling them to regain control of their thoughts and emotions. By repeatedly listening to recorded affirmations, meditating, or creating visualisations, the mind becomes accustomed to the words and images and can use them as a distraction when faced with fear or anxiety. Using practical techniques and self-hypnosis, you can learn to manage your fear, overcome anxiety, and regain control.

Childhood anxiety and related disorders link strongly with parental influence, as adults' modelling and response to fear can significantly affect children's fear responses. The fear response is triggered by the sympathetic branch of the autonomic nervous system, resulting in a series of physiological changes that can override conscious decision-making. However, resilience is crucial in managing anxiety and overcoming fear. It empowers individuals to recover from fear and bounce back from difficult experiences, altering the autonomic nervous system's response and enabling individuals to confront their fears with courage and strength. Developing resilience is a process that requires training and practice, preventing individuals from being trapped in the freeze, or fawn response and significantly impacting their fear response.

Fear can be an emotion that prevents us from achieving our goals, but it can be managed and overcome with the right tools. One technique that has been particularly effective in helping clients address their fears is inner child healing. By accessing and healing past emotional wounds from childhood, the negative thought patterns and beliefs holding you back can be identified and released, allowing you to move forward with self-awareness, self-compassion, and confidence.

Through inner child healing and other self-healing practices, clients have developed a deeper understanding of themselves and their fears, allowing them to break free and achieve their goals. Building resilience empowers individuals to overcome their fears and manage anxiety. A good case example is that of AJ, who had a phobia of dogs due to a traumatic experience in her childhood. At three years old, AJ was attacked by a dog, leading to a fear that caused her to avoid places where she might encounter dogs. This fear made it challenging for her to participate in normal daily activities.

However, with the support of her mother and involvement in a martial arts group that trained with dogs, AJ was able to confront her fear and develop resilience. At first, AJ met both trainer and dog under duress, as they were invited to speak at her school. But her mother realised that AJ did not want to cause a scene and sat through the assembly without displaying fear. Slowly, AJ began to develop a friendship with the dog, as the trainer and dog attended an after-school club. This experience empowered AJ to respond with the fight response, which enabled her to manage her anxiety and overcome her fear of dogs. AJ's story demonstrates the transformative power of resilience and how it can help individuals manage anxiety and overcome their fears through exposure.

As I write this, I recall some of my most daunting experiences. One time, while travelling with my mother, sister, and cousin (who happened to be a Lieutenant General in the Indian army), we found ourselves in a remote region in the mountains of India. Suddenly, the soldiers had to hide us from bandits, and fear set in. At that moment, we were completely vulnerable, and I could feel my body respond with the flight, fight, and freeze response. However, the bravery and resilience of those soldiers in protecting us were remarkable. They risked their own lives to keep us safe, and that experience left an indelible impression on me.

Similarly, I accidentally walked into the occupied Green Line area while living and working in Cyprus. A Turkish soldier pointed a gun at me, and fear washed over me like a wave. It was a daunting experience, and my body responded with the flight, fight, and freeze response again. However, I refused to let fear take control and decided to push forward. I demonstrated resilience and courage, despite my heart racing and my palms sweating. Looking back, I realise that these experiences have taught me valuable lessons about fear, resilience, and the power of the flight, fight, freeze and fawn responses.

Developing Resilience

Fear and resilience are intimately connected, as we have seen through AJ's story and my own experiences. When individuals face traumatic incidents or serious trauma, the autonomic nervous system's response including flight, fight, freeze, or fawn can take over, leaving them feeling fearless. However, we can train ourselves to change our body's response to non-life-threatening stressors by developing resilience. For example, AJ's story illustrates how her mother's support and involvement in a martial arts group empowered her to confront her fears and build strength, enabling her to respond with a fight response. Similarly, when I faced life-threatening situations, such as being hidden from bandits in India and exploring the occupied Green Line area in Cyprus, I refused to let fear limit me and developed resilience through continued travel and facing my fears head-on.

My childhood was full of resilience-building lessons. I learned to confront my fears and assess situations in the moment. This mindset enabled me to face challenges with courage and strength and overcome obstacles that once seemed insurmountable. Developing resilience is an ongoing process that can significantly impact an individual's ability to manage anxiety and overcome fear.

Overcoming fear is a challenging journey that requires perseverance, empathy, and the courage to confront your anxieties head-on. Resilience is key to managing anxiety and facing your fears with strength and determination. To cultivate resilience, you must proactively manage your anxiety, seek professional help, and build a strong support network of friends and family. By acknowledging that fear is a natural part of life and learning to embrace it as a challenge rather than a threat, you can develop the mindset necessary to confront your fears with courage and fortitude. By doing so, you can navigate life's twists and turns with greater ease, find strength in the face of adversity, and uncover your true potential.

Resilience is key to managing fear and anxiety, but it cannot eliminate the possibility of experiencing these emotions. Fear is a natural response to stressful situations, and resilience will allow you to handle it effectively by manipulating your thoughts and coping mechanisms. However, we must recognise that the fear responses of others can influence our own fear responses. My mother's remarkable resilience in facing her fears and anxieties served as an inspiration for me. She embraced life and took risks, despite losing my father and her subsequent concerns at such a young age. She was widowed at the age of only 32, my father was 38. Her resilience was a reminder that overcoming difficult situations with strength and courage is possible, setting an example for those around us.

In Chapter 5, I shared my grief during IVF treatment. A significant miscarriage and subsequent life-threatening surgery brought my past fears and anxieties to the forefront. When my husband left me, several aspects of my life fell apart, leading to a domino effect. My fear of being alone became unbearable, and new fears (such as heights and the sea) emerged. Even the thought of travelling alone left me paranoid and anxious. While fear of the unknown is natural, my concern for the grief others might experience is even greater than my own.

Scott Burrows, a renowned motivational speaker and author, exemplifies resilience and grit through his personal story of perseverance.

In his book, Burrows chronicles his extraordinary journey from paralysis to walking, offering readers an intimate look into his struggles and triumphs. Following a life-altering car accident at age 19, doctors told Scott that he would never regain the ability to walk. However, Scott's refusal to accept this fate propelled him towards intense physical therapy and a steadfast belief in his own recovery. Through visualisation and unyielding perseverance, he defied the odds, gradually regaining sensation in his legs and ultimately achieving the remarkable feat of walking again with the aid of a walker. Scott's story serves as a beacon of inspiration, motivating individuals to overcome their own obstacles and never give up on their dreams (Burrows, 2013). By sharing his experiences, Scott offers a powerful message of hope and resilience, reminding us that we possess the inner strength to triumph over adversity and embrace a future without fear, but instead filled with limitless possibilities.

Practising Control Over Fear

Practising techniques to control my nervousness, such as removing myself emotionally and psychologically from my fear, helps me focus on something more pleasant and present. I try to focus on something that makes me feel safe and relaxed, which is essential for exploring my fears. Questioning all my emotions would only exacerbate my anxiety, and the more anxious I become, the more my past stories surface to explain why I might feel the way I do. Overcoming fear requires self-compassion and empathy, and by asking ourselves simple questions and focusing on what makes us feel safe, we can avoid extreme fear and continue to develop our resilience.

You must stop yourself in your tracks to avoid spiralling into chronic fear. As I began trying to conceive, I faced a persistent fear of infertility that caused me anxiety. I was stuck in a vicious circle, unable to let go of the emotions preventing me from successfully conceiving. Overcoming chronic fear and anxiety requires a deep understanding of these emotions. Fear and anxiety are stored as stories in the *basal ganglia*, a cluster of nuclei that control behaviour, eye movement, learning procedures for habitual behaviours, and cognitive functions. Our brains are wired to create a feeling primarily intended to protect us and make us feel secure, but sometimes this feeling can lead to chronic fear and anxiety. The longer we experience these emotions, the worse our overall health becomes.

The cerebellum in our brains allows us to recall how our body reacted when we experienced fear in the past. When our minds realise that we are not in danger, it causes our emotions to drain the body's self-healing mechanisms, and before we know it, our self-preservation mechanisms have been damaged. This cycle can be exhausting and damaging to our overall health. As I experienced first-hand during my IVF treatment, the best way to overcome chronic fear is to create better stories in our minds that can replace harmful thoughts stored in our central nervous system from the past.

Our responses to fear, flight, fight, freeze and fawn can significantly impact our situations. Setting healthy boundaries and reflecting on and letting go of past events can help us progress, just as Sara and Scott did. We can use our resilience to manage fear and anxiety, turning them into strengths. It is important to be kind to ourselves during moments of fear and anxiety, practice techniques to control nervousness, and focus on what makes us feel safe and relaxed. By being aware of our fear responses and acknowledging how others influence them, we can better manage our fears and cultivate resilience. Through self-compassion, self-hypnosis, visualisation, relaxation, asking yourself simple questions, and soothing self-talk, you can avoid extreme fear and continue to grow and develop your resilience.

Controlling fear is challenging, but it is a skill that can be learned through positive self-talk and visualisation techniques. It may take time and practice to overcome fear and anxiety, but once you know the tools, you can use them to overcome the emotions that have been holding you back. The key is to become aware of your thoughts and feelings and take control of them, instead of letting them control you.

Fix Me Tools

Use Meditation. Practising meditation helps you become more aware of your thoughts and emotions. It also helps you achieve a state of calmness and relaxation, which reduces the amount of stress hormones such as cortisol in your body. In addition, regular meditation helps you develop the ability to pause and assess the situation when you feel threatened, rather than reacting automatically.

Create a Vision Board. Visualise your desired outcome and consciously choose your thoughts to overcome emotional obstacles. By creating powerful memories in your nervous system, you replace negative limiting beliefs with positive ones. Allow synaptic pathways to form in your emotional memory centre, making positive emotions more prominent than negative ones. Visualise the life you want to manifest and let your vision board serve as a visual representation of your goals, dreams, and aspirations. By actively engaging in this practice, you harness the power of visualisation to shape your reality and move closer to achieving your desired outcomes.

Practise Repetition. Creating new memories and pathways in your brain requires repetition. Practising mindfulness and visualisation regularly is essential to create lasting change in your nervous system. By repeating positive affirmations and visualisations, you rewire your brain to respond positively to situations that once caused fear and anxiety.

Make Mindful Choices. Being mindful of the stories in your mind and the experiences that have influenced them is an essential step in controlling your fear. You can let go of negative beliefs and create positive memories by being aware of your thoughts. Use positive affirmations and words in your mind, so there is more practice of positive self-talk. You can also surround yourself with positive influences, such as inspirational stories and supportive people.

Use Positive Visualisation. Scott Burrows' story is a prime example of the power of positive visualisation. He could eventually stand and walk again, never losing sight of his walking ability. Positive visualisation can help you overcome the emotional obstacles affecting your quality of life. It involves creating powerful memories in your nervous system to replace negative limiting beliefs.

In conclusion, I hope you have explored the intricate relationship between fear, resilience, and the fight–flight–freeze and fawn responses. By understanding the physiological and psychological aspects of fear, you have gained valuable insights into how traumatic experiences can shape your fear responses and trigger anxiety disorders. Through the development of resilience, you have learned that managing fear and anxiety in healthy and constructive ways is possible. By practising self-awareness, seeking support, and utilising effective coping strategies such as self-hypnosis, visualisation, and positive self-talk, you can overcome fear, cultivate resilience, and embrace a life filled with courage, strength, and personal growth. Remember, you can confront your fears, control your responses, and create a future free from the limitations of fear and anxiety.

References

Bradford, W. (1920). The physiological response to stress: The foundation of the autonomic nervous system. *Journal of Comparative Neurology*, 30(1), 45–62.

Burrows, S. (2013). *Vision Mindset Grit: How to Stand Up When Life Paralyses You!* eBookIt.com

Cannon, W. B. (1915). *Bodily Changes in Pain, Hunger, Fear and Rage.* New York: Appleton.

Lazarus, R. S. and Folkman, S. (1984). *Stress, Appraisal, and Coping.* New York: Springer.

Walker, P. (2013). *Complex PTSD: From Surviving to Thriving.* Create-Space Independent Publishing Platform.

8

Self-Sabotaging Behaviour

....

In the last chapter, we looked at how fear can hold us back and prevent us from achieving our goals and aspirations. Although fear can be a healthy and helpful emotion, it can also become your worst enemy, leading to feelings of anxiety, stress, and self-doubt. In this chapter, I will focus on the relationship between anxiety and self-sabotage, exploring how these two conditions are intertwined and the impact they can have on your life.

Anxiety and self-sabotage often go hand in hand, with you feeling anxious and engaging in behaviours that sabotage your progress and prevent you from achieving your goals. You may procrastinate, avoid tasks, and engage in negative self-talk. Moreover, these self-sabotaging behaviours can also trigger feelings of anxiety, creating a vicious cycle that is difficult for you to break free from.

Understanding the connection between anxiety and self-sabotage allows you to break this cycle and regain control over your thoughts and behaviours. You can engage in self-reflection and utilise other techniques to recognise when you are using self-sabotaging behaviours and take steps towards addressing them. With the right tools and support, you can overcome anxiety and self-sabotage and move towards a successful life.

I have worked with several high-profile individuals, including a celebrity, let's call him Max, who struggled with self-sabotage throughout his career. Despite achieving success in Hollywood, he often felt like a failure and engaged in behaviours that undermined his accomplishments. This is common; most who self-sabotage do so due to fears of failure, fears of success, and low self-worth or self-esteem, which lead them to engage in behaviours that hinder their progress. Max was prevented from reaching his goals, and this is a common experience among those who struggle with anxiety and self-sabotage—regardless of their level of success or notoriety. Recognising and addressing these behaviour patterns is essential to achieve your goals and live a fulfilling life. You can understand the underlying causes of your behaviour and work to overcome them, breaking free from self-sabotage and moving forward with greater confidence, self-awareness, and self-acceptance. In the following sections, I will explore the relationship between anxiety and self-sabotage, and techniques for overcoming these behaviour patterns.

Unveiling Self-Sabotaging Behaviour

Self-sabotage is a typical behaviour that can hinder you from achieving your goals or fulfilling your potential. It manifests in various ways, such as procrastination, negative self-talk, self-doubt, fear of failure or success, and self-destructive behaviours. These behaviours often stem from limiting beliefs and negative thought patterns that consume your mind and control your development based on past experiences and conditioning. Therefore, self-sabotage holds you back from living an abundant life and achieving your dreams because you feel overwhelmed by uncertainty and doubt.

Breaking down significant concerns into manageable parts is an effective strategy for dealing with overwhelming issues. It helps if you separate the aspects of a problem within your control from those that are not. By focusing on what you can change and developing strategies to overcome negative thought patterns and behaviours, you can break free from self-sabotaging patterns and achieve your desired outcomes. This approach will help you take small steps towards your goals, build confidence and momentum, and treat yourself with kindness and compassion. Ultimately, by staying committed to your goals and persevering through challenges, you can break free from self-sabotage and succeed personally and professionally.

Max, although a talented Hollywood actor, struggled with a profound fear of failure and rejection that was holding him back in his career. He firmly believed that avoiding disappointment was the only path to success, leading him to consistently avoid auditions, even those with great career potential. As a result, despite his undeniable talent, he found himself trapped in a cycle of self-sabotage, causing his career to stagnate. Aware of the need for change, Max sought my guidance and our journey began.

The Journey of Self-Reflection

As Max's therapist, I worked closely with him to identify and challenge the negative thought patterns and beliefs fuelling his anxiety. We meticulously broke down his significant concerns into manageable parts, aiming to develop strategies to help him overcome his self-sabotaging behaviours and thought patterns. Through our sessions, Max gradually learnt to reframe his thinking and develop effective coping mechanisms to manage anxiety better.

During Max's therapeutic journey, we engaged in self-reflection to identify the root causes of his fear of failure and rejection. Through open and honest dialogue, Max gained valuable insights into his limiting beliefs and negative thought patterns, which traced back to his experiences of failure at school. These academic setbacks profoundly impacted his self-esteem and confidence, leading him to develop a deep-seated fear of failure. Max constantly worried about the potential negative outcomes and consequences of any endeavour he pursued, fearing that it would result in rejection and judgement from others. As we explored Max's experiences and emotions surrounding his academic challenges, we discovered that he associated failure with personal inadequacy, believing that his worth and value were tied to his academic performance. These beliefs shaped his perception of himself and instilled a pervasive fear of failure in various aspects of his life. However, through our therapeutic conversations, Max gradually gained a new perspective. He realised that failure could be an opportunity for growth and learning rather than a reflection of his worth. We worked together to challenge his negative perceptions and reframe his thoughts, encouraging him to shift his inner dialogue from "what if it fails?" to "what if it works?". By taking small steps and setting realistic goals, you can actively explore your desired outcomes and the positive possibilities arising from your efforts.

Max started to build a more positive and empowering mindset. He learned to challenge his self-doubt and embrace the potential for success, gradually transforming his fear of failure into a driving force for personal growth. By acknowledging the root causes of his fear, particularly his experiences of failure at school, Max embarked on a transformative journey of self-discovery, gaining confidence and resilience along the way. With unwavering determination and a newfound resilience, Max began to experience breakthroughs. His hard work and perseverance led to him securing a significant role in a highly acclaimed film. This was a testament to his remarkable growth and transformation, as he realised he could achieve his dreams and reach his full potential as an actor by confronting his fears head-on, letting go of things that did not serve a purpose, and developing coping strategies.

So how did he do it? First, Max demonstrated the power of setting clear goals and breaking them down into manageable steps. Next, he identified specific auditions he wanted to pursue and meticulously outlined the necessary preparations, creating a roadmap for success. This process provided Max with a clear direction and a sense of purpose, which fuelled his motivation to take action and avoid the pitfalls of procrastination. By focusing on specific tasks and mapping out a path towards his goals, Max stayed motivated and made consistent progress towards achieving his desired outcomes. Furthermore, Max recognised the value of accountability and support in maintaining his motivation. As a result, he shared his goals and progress with his family and me. An external support system was vital in keeping Max motivated and focused, providing him with the necessary feedback, reassurance, and structure to stay on track and avoid procrastination. As a result,

Max continues to thrive in his career without therapy or a coach. And since then, he has been successfully appearing on our screens.

Max's story is a powerful reminder that even without access to therapy, you possess the inherent capacity for self-reflection, perseverance, and a willingness to confront your fears. When faced with significant concerns and self-sabotaging patterns, you can still embark on a journey of personal growth by breaking down these concerns into manageable parts. Through self-reflection, you can identify the negative thought patterns and behaviours holding you back and develop strategies to challenge and overcome them. This requires resilience, determination, and a commitment to self-improvement. By embracing this mindset, you can tap into your inner strength and reach your full potential, transcending the limitations that may come from a lack of professional support.

It is essential to delve into your behaviours' underlying causes and triggers to combat self-sabotage and anxiety. Take the time to reflect on your past experiences and ask yourself difficult questions. What are your true aspirations and purpose in life? Do you feel motivated to pursue them, or lack the drive? By honestly addressing these questions, you will gain a deeper understanding of your inner desires and the obstacles that may hold you back.

In a remarkable case, I worked with another high-profile client, Shar. She is a princess of a foreign country who struggles with self-sabotage and anxiety in her long-term relationship. Despite being engaged, she constantly questioned her worth, which led to withheld anger and a recurring cycle of self-doubt. This manifested in defensive behaviours that created unnecessary issues in her relationship. Through therapy, Shar embarked on a life-changing journey of self-reflection, where she bravely confronted her negative thought patterns and learned to manage her emotions.

With therapy support, Shar gained self-awareness and discovered powerful techniques to redirect her irrational thoughts towards positive perspectives. She actively challenged her beliefs about her current relationship, reframing her mindset from dread and judgement due to past negative experiences. Instead, she began recognising her accomplishments and strengths, consciously comparing the positive aspects of her life to the negative ones. Over time, this gradual shift in thinking led to tangible changes in her behaviours and emotions.

Shar's journey towards overcoming self-sabotage and anxiety was fuelled by her newfound motivation and a sense of purpose. Through self-reflection, she realised she was not ready to marry, not because of any fault in her partner, but because she lacked self-love. This realisation allowed her to prioritise her needs and desires, and she began building a healthy relationship with herself. By setting clear goals aligned with her aspirations and celebrating her successes, Shar cultivated self-confidence and avoided self-judgement and procrastination. She also learned to break down larger objectives into smaller, achievable milestones, which helped her stay focused and motivated. With therapy guidance, Shar bravely confronted her self-doubt, and through open and honest communication with her partner, she expressed her feelings, concerns, and desires. Shar ensured that her needs and limitations were respected by setting and maintaining clear boundaries. Furthermore, she understood the importance of self-care and prioritised it, engaging in activities that nourished her physically, mentally, and emotionally. With these steps, Shar enriched a deep sense of self-love, purpose, and motivation, and ultimately reached a point where she felt ready to pursue the idea of marriage, knowing that she had built a solid foundation within herself.

The Value of Introspection and Finding Purpose

Overcoming anxiety and self-sabotage entails a holistic and comprehensive approach that goes beyond traditional strategies. It requires leveraging one's current circumstances, introspecting on personal behaviours, and understanding their impact on individual goals and aspirations. Instead of seeking external validation, the emphasis shifts towards recognising your intrinsic worth and unique abilities, disregarding the opinions or influences of others.

In Shar's case, therapy provided a nurturing and supportive environment for profound self-reflection. Within this therapeutic space, she bravely confronted her negative thoughts and embraced her anxiety, using them as catalysts for personal development and evolution. As a result, Shar attained personal fulfilment and deepened her connections by effectively managing her emotions, discovering fresh motivation and purpose, and seeking the necessary support to navigate her challenges.

During therapy, Shar unearthed a latent passion for fashion design and felt a profound calling to contribute to charitable causes. This realisation became a driving force in her journey towards self-actualisation. Her experiences are a powerful example of therapy's ability to dismantle self-sabotaging patterns and conquer anxiety. It underscores the importance of introspection, nurturing emotional intelligence to regulate distressing emotions, reframing cognitive patterns that hinder progress, and fostering intrinsic motivation and a sense of purpose.

By delving into the psychological dynamics of Shar's journey, we gain an appreciation for the significance of her therapeutic process. Through introspection, she gained insight into her thought processes, emotional triggers, and behavioural patterns perpetuating self-sabotage and anxiety. This newfound awareness empowered her to challenge and transform those patterns, gradually replacing them with healthier, more constructive alternatives. Moreover, by embracing her anxiety and perceiving it as an opportunity for personal growth, Shar harnessed its energy to propel herself forward.

Shar's journey highlights therapy's profound impact on an individual's ability to overcome self-sabotage and anxiety. It illuminates the potential for profound personal development through self-reflection, emotional management, cognitive reframing, and cultivating motivation and purpose. By engaging in this multifaceted process, individuals can liberate themselves from self-imposed limitations, embrace their true potential, and embark on a path of personal flourishing and self-fulfilment.

The concept of purpose can sometimes be misunderstood as a rigid adherence to a predetermined path, creating feelings of being overwhelmed and restricted. However, the essence of purpose lies in embracing creativity and growth rather than confining oneself to a fixed trajectory. Discovering purpose involves embarking on a journey of self-exploration, delving deep within to unearth the passions that truly ignite the soul and align with your core values. This process of introspection and self-discovery is crucial in fostering a sense of meaning and direction in life.

Individuals with a clear and defined sense of purpose find it easier to set meaningful goals and navigate away from self-sabotaging behaviours. The objective is a guiding light, illuminating the path and influencing actions and decisions. It infuses intentionality into every endeavour, lending a sense of significance. By having a clear sense of purpose, you will experience a profound sense of accomplishment while also finding solace in alleviating anxiety, arising from having a clear sense of direction and empowerment.

Delving into this phenomenon, we discover that having a sense of purpose profoundly impacts mental well-being. When individuals live with a clear understanding of purpose, their actions become imbued with intention and meaning. This alignment between intent and action cultivates a sense of coherence and satisfaction, contributing to overall mental wellness. Moreover, finding purpose unlocks an individual's full potential. When a deep sense of purpose drives your pursuits, you are more likely to engage in activities that resonate with your authentic self. This alignment between purpose and passion creates a heightened sense of self-fulfilment and personal growth. Pursuing a goal creates a positive feedback loop, reinforcing your determination and increasing overall well-being.

It is essential to recognise that discovering purpose is not a static process but an emotional journey of self-discovery and adaptation. As you evolve and grow, your sense of purpose may also develop. Embracing this fluidity and allowing room for exploration and growth will enable you to live more intentionally and authentically, fostering greater satisfaction and overall well-being.

Anyone can embark on a transformative journey of self-discovery and growth by actively engaging in self-therapy and incorporating various techniques. For instance, exploring your creativity can be a powerful form of self-expression and healing. Like Shar, you can engage in creative activities such as drawing, painting, writing, or playing music, allowing you to express your thoughts and emotions freely. Creative outlets provide a safe space to explore your inner world, tap into your unique perspectives, and gain a deeper understanding of yourself. Additionally, consider engaging in charitable or volunteer work. Giving back to the community contributes to a greater sense of resolution and allows you to connect with others, develop empathy, and gain a broader perspective. Through these profound self-therapeutic endeavours, you can nurture your personal growth, foster inner strength, and embark on a remarkable voyage towards a more meaningful and rewarding existence.

Life is rarely a smooth journey, and I have come to understand this truth all too well. There are moments when everything is falling into place, only for unexpected waves of emotion to hinder our progress. These waves often originate from the words we hear in our minds. Self-criticism is a common tendency we all experience, where we may label ourselves foolish or inadequate. While I discourage self-deprecating language, it is important to acknowledge that occasional self-criticism may arise, especially when we feel embarrassed or disappointed. I so often hear people mumble, "That was stupid of me". However, the key lies in recognising that self-compassion should take precedence over self-sabotage, and replacing negative words with "We all make mistakes" being kinder towards yourself—is a healthier option.

To embark on this transformative shift, we must diligently promote the invaluable trait of self-awareness, which guides our journey towards self-compassion and liberation from self-sabotage. This entails a courageous exploration of our behaviours, including those contributing to our hindrances. In this process, we uncover the depths of our aspirations and intentions by carefully reflecting on our past experiences and engaging in profound introspective questioning.

Through this introspection, we will unravel the intricate details of our true desires, peering into the depths of our being to understand the driving forces within us. This clarity empowers us to confront the obstacles that obstruct our path, converting them into stepping stones on our transformative journey. It is crucial to embrace the multifaceted nature of our existence, knowing that we are comprised of both light and shadow, strength and vulnerability. Accepting the entirety of our being the good, the bad, and the ugly enables us to find equilibrium and inner harmony.

In this pursuit of self-awareness, we learn to discern the aspects of ourselves that serve our highest potential and those that undermine it. This discernment becomes the compass guiding our choices and actions, aligning them with our authentic selves. By striking this delicate balance, we can navigate the complexities of our inner landscape with grace and wisdom, allowing us to embrace our imperfections while continuously striving for growth and self-improvement.

The journey towards self-compassion and liberation from self-sabotage requires unwavering commitment and dedication. It demands that we embrace the truth of who we are, acknowledging both our strengths and weaknesses without judgement or self-condemnation. Through this self-acceptance, we create a fertile ground for change and profound healing.

Effectively managing your emotions is paramount in overcoming self-sabotaging tendencies. Rather than suppressing emotions like anxiety, anger, or worthlessness, allowing them to surface and acknowledging their presence is vital. Please pay attention to warning signs indicating when emotions are becoming overwhelming and develop healthy coping mechanisms to manage and redirect them constructively. Engaging in deep breathing exercises, embracing creative outlets, and seeking support from trusted individuals are all valuable approaches to effectively navigate and channel emotions.

Cognitive reframing constitutes a powerful technique in combating self-sabotage by challenging irrational thoughts and negative thinking patterns. Recognise when your inner dialogue becomes irrational and consciously redirect your thoughts towards more positive and empowering perspectives. Maintaining a journal can aid in capturing negative thoughts, enabling you to counter them with evidence of your accomplishments, strengths, and past successes. By consciously comparing the positive aspects of your life to the negative ones, you will gradually reshape your mindset, fostering a more optimistic outlook.

Motivation and purpose are integral in breaking free from self-sabotage and avoiding procrastination. Start by defining your ideas about how you wish to live your life and what you want from it. How you envision yourself, others, and your environment. What is your role in your family and community? Next, identify the values, passions, and long-term goals that drive you. Subsequently, break down these goals into smaller, realistic milestones, and remember to celebrate your achievements along the way. This process fuels motivation and supports self-confidence as you witness your progress towards your desired outcomes.

Conquering self-sabotage and anxiety requires a comprehensive approach encompassing self-awareness, emotional management, cognitive reframing, motivation, and purpose. By nurturing these areas and implementing tailored strategies, you will empower yourself to transcend self-sabotaging patterns and achieve personal and professional fulfilment. You can confidently navigate the path towards a rewarding and purposeful life through persistent effort, self-reflection, and unwavering faith in your unique abilities.

Fix Me Tools

Nurture Self-Value and Recognise Your Skillset. Appreciating and recognising your skillset is essential to overcoming self-sabotage. A pivotal approach to appreciating your abilities and skills is to consistently practice self-acknowledgement and celebrate your accomplishments, regardless of their magnitude. Dedicate daily moments to reflect on your achievements, talents, and progress, expressing genuine gratitude for your unique creativity. You will nurture a positive and empowering self-perception by consciously recognising and appreciating your capabilities. This process enhances self-confidence and serves as a catalyst for continuous personal growth and success. Embrace the inherent worth you hold, independent of external validation or influence, and bask in understanding the value you bring to any situation. Honouring your unique strengths, talents, and experiences amplifies self-value and creates a solid foundation for overcoming self-sabotage.

Embrace Intrinsic Motivation. Motivation is a powerful force that can propel or hold us back. Instead of relying solely on external factors for motivation, tap into your intrinsic drivers. Define your purpose, values, and long-term goals. Identify what truly excites and energises you. By aligning your actions with your inner passions and values, you can foster sustainable motivation that will help you stay focused and committed.

Set Realistic Goals and Avoid Procrastination. Break your goals into smaller, manageable, attainable, and realistic tasks. This will allow you to progress incrementally, increasing your sense of achievement and maintaining momentum. Additionally, develop strategies to avoid procrastination. Prioritise tasks, schedule, and establish accountability measures to keep yourself on track. Remember, taking consistent action, even in small steps, is key to overcoming self-sabotage.

Challenge Negative Thought Patterns. Our thoughts shape our reality, and negative thought patterns can contribute to anxiety and self-sabotage. Challenge and reframe these negative thoughts by examining the evidence supporting them. Substitute them with more positive, empowering thoughts and affirmations. Engage in self-compassion to cultivate a healthier and more optimistic mindset.

Manage Emotions and Build Resilience. Anxiety often stems from a fear of the unfamiliar and a lack of control. Practice emotional regulation techniques such as deep meditation, breathing, or journalling to manage anxiety and stress. Build emotional resilience by developing coping mechanisms and seeking support from professional resources or loved ones. Remember that emotions are temporary, and by learning to navigate and process them, you can maintain focus and make clearer decisions.

Embrace Imperfection and Learn from Setbacks. Perfectionism can fuel self-sabotage by setting unrealistic expectations and fostering fear of failure. Adopt the idea that mistakes and setbacks are part of the learning process. Implement a growth mindset and view challenges as opportunities for growth and self-improvement. Learn from your experiences and apply the lessons to future endeavours.

Overcoming anxiety and self-sabotage is a journey of self-discovery and personal growth. By recognising your own worth, embracing intrinsic motivation, setting realistic goals, challenging negative thoughts, managing emotions, and embracing imperfection, you can break free from self-sabotaging patterns and create a life of purpose and success. Remember that change takes time and effort, but perseverance and belief in your abilities can overcome self-sabotage and anxiety and unlock your true potential.

9

Jealousy and Anxiety

In the previous chapter, we delved into the intricacies of self-sabotage and anxiety, uncovering how these challenges impact our lives. Building upon that foundation, I now focus on the complex landscape of jealousy. This chapter will explore jealousy in depth, shedding light on its multifaceted nature and profound influence on your relationships and personal well-being.

With its intricate web of emotions and triggers, jealousy presents a unique challenge to explore and understand. Its complexities stem from many factors, including comparison, insecurity, fear of rejection or abandonment, and societal pressures. To delve into these complexities, I will examine case examples and practical strategies to unravel the intricate threads of jealousy and provide insights for growth and healing.

To begin your journey, we must explore the nature of jealousy, uncovering its triggers and the underlying psychological and emotional drivers that give rise to its presence in your life. By gaining a more profound understanding of jealousy, you can develop a more nuanced perspective, allowing you to navigate its complexities with greater insight and compassion. Let us embark on this exploration with open minds and hearts, ready to uncover the wisdom and growth ahead.

To illustrate the impact of jealousy, let's consider the case of Ronaldo, a regular student and client of mine who has gained online fame as an influencer. As Ronaldo's social media following grew, he became increasingly consumed by jealousy. Immersed in a world of carefully curated perfection, he started comparing himself to other influencers and feeling inadequate and envious, especially of those with fewer followers who were verified account holders. Jealousy distorted his perception, leading him to engage in toxic online behaviour, such as leaving hateful comments and acting like a troll. Ronaldo's case exemplifies how jealousy, fuelled by comparison and insecurities, can drive individuals to harmful actions in their quest for validation.

Understanding the triggers of jealousy, both in the digital realm and beyond, is crucial for addressing its hold on us. As Ronaldo's therapist, I guided him through the intricate landscape of his anxiety and jealousy. Together, we embarked on a therapeutic journey to understand the underlying causes and develop healthier coping strategies. It became evident that Ronaldo's jealousy stemmed from deep-rooted insecurities and fears of inadequacy. He constantly compared himself to other influencers, experiencing envy and self-doubt when observing their seemingly perfect lives and success on social media. This comparison fuelled his anxieties, distorting his perception of reality and leading to toxic thinking and behaviour patterns.

Ronaldo experienced a profound transformation throughout our therapeutic sessions, as he embarked on self-discovery and growth. Drawing on an eclectic approach to therapy, including elements of dialectical behaviour therapy (DBT), we delved into the underlying patterns and influences that shaped Ronaldo's behaviour. For example, we explored how his tendency to engage in people-pleasing stems from his upbringing, where he felt the need to constantly please his elder sister, who took on a parental role due to his feeling abandoned by his parents and searching for attention. Through this exploration, Ronaldo gained valuable insights into his past and its impact on his present experiences. Moreover, incorporating mindfulness exercises within DBT proved instrumental in Ronaldo's journey, as he learnt to disengage from anxious and jealous thoughts, gaining a deeper understanding of his emotions and cultivating a more objective perspective. Additionally, the DBT skills training equipped Ronaldo with effective communication strategies and assertiveness skills, enabling him to express his needs, set boundaries, and navigate conflicts confidently and clearly. Ronaldo's increased self-awareness and prioritisation of his well-being allowed him to move away from the "fawn" response, as discussed briefly in Chapter 7, which he had adopted to appease his sister. This transformative process empowered Ronaldo to foster healthier relationships, develop resilience in jealousy and anxiety, and embrace a more authentic and nourishing life.

Another similar case occurred in the context of my therapeutic sessions. Nicky is a very passionate and exceptionally talented artist and client. However, he grappled with jealousy as he compared his artwork to that of his peers. Recognising the need for self-exploration and self-compassion, we embarked on a transposing journey. We discovered that Nicky's jealousy stemmed from his tendency to seek external validation and measure his worth based on the recognition and success of others.

To address this challenge, we employed strategies designed to redirect Nicky's focus and foster a sense of self-appreciation. Through our therapeutic sessions, Nicky discovered the therapeutic value of self-expression and self-admiration by embracing new mediums and pushing his artistic boundaries. Instead of being consumed by self-criticism, he learnt to appreciate his unique style and creative journey, finding satisfaction independent of external comparisons.

Furthermore, as I observed Nicky's vibrant personality, I recognised his inherent gift of humour. Recognising the profound impact laughter could have on his journey, I encouraged the exploration of laughter therapy as a significant catalyst for his change. Together, we delved into the mesmerising power of humour and light-heartedness, seeking ways that Nicky could harness its magic to enhance his well-being and infuse his artistic expression with joy and playfulness.

In our quest to unravel the mysteries of laughter, we discovered its incredible power to create a chemical change within us. When we experience genuine laughter, it sets off a beautiful symphony of neurotransmitters—chemical releases that flow through our body, bringing about a delightful cascade of positive effects. Endorphins (nature's pain relievers) are one of these magical neurotransmitters. As endorphins spread throughout our system, they create a euphoric wave of well-being, easing our physical and emotional state. They effortlessly melt away the pain, release tension, and invite profound relaxation into our entire being.

Meanwhile, dopamine, the captivating neurotransmitter of pleasure and reward, joins the performance. With its joyful embrace, dopamine uplifts our spirits, kindling motivation and infusing our inner world with an intoxicating blend of joy and excitement. Moreover, its presence catalyses an optimistic outlook, nourishing our sense of pleasure and amplifying the vibrancy of life itself.

Adding to this symphony of chemical marvels, serotonin steps onto the stage, gracing us with its radiant presence. Known as the "happy hormone", serotonin is vital in harmonising your mood and emotional well-being. When laughter stirs its release, a sense of serenity and improved attitude envelops you, enhancing your social bonds and fostering a deepened understanding of connection with others. It weaves empathy, solidarity, and belonging, painting your life with the hues of shared laughter.

This marvellous interplay of chemical conversion brought about by laughter can uplift your spirits and bestow a myriad of physiological and psychological benefits upon you. It becomes a balm for the mind and body, nourishing your immune system, reducing stress levels, lowering blood pressure, and cultivating profound well-being. For Nicky, embracing the path of laughter therapy allowed him to unlock the transcendent potential of humour. Through laughter, yoga, companionship with those who spark joy, and indulging in comedy shows, he immersed himself in a symphony of endorphins, dopamine, and serotonin. These magical chemical companions guided him to a profound shift in mindset, breathing renewed vitality and an irresistible zest for life into his creative endeavours.

Recognising the significance of a supportive network, Nicky sought fellow artists who would share in celebrating and appreciating each other's work. Engaging in constructive discussions and collaborative projects, and providing feedback within this community, allowed Nicky to establish a sense of belonging and inspiration. In addition, the presence of like-minded individuals who uplift and encourage one another created a nurturing environment that minimised the space for jealousy to thrive.

I emphasise the practice of self-reflection and gratitude as powerful tools for refining a mindset of abundance and contentment. Nicky reflected on his artistic journey, acknowledging his progress, unique style, and personal accomplishments. Through gratitude exercises, such as maintaining a gratitude journal or expressing appreciation for his artistic achievements, Nicky fostered a sense of fulfilment and diminished the impact of jealousy. These practices allowed him to approach his creative endeavours with renewed appreciation and self-worth.

Playing the Comparison Game

The journeys of Ronaldo and Nicky offer poignant insights into the pervasive phenomenon of what is sometimes referred to as "comparisonitis", which lies at the heart of jealousy. Comparisonitis, characterised by the relentless comparison of oneself to others, tends to ignite envy and a sense of inadequacy. Ronaldo and Nicky confronted this challenge, grappling with feelings of jealousy even as accomplished individuals within their respective fields. Despite their achievements, they realised that relying on external validation alone is insufficient to measure true self-worth. In their pursuit of personal growth, they embarked on self-discovery and self-appreciation, and most of all self-acceptance. They learnt to cherish their unique strengths and accomplishments, regardless of how they stacked up against others. By shifting their focus inward, Ronaldo and Nicky nurtured a profound sense of self-worth that transcends the trappings of comparison. Through this empowering journey, they emerged as individuals celebrating their own unique qualities, free from the chains of jealousy and the limitations of external benchmarks.

Central to the journeys of Ronaldo and Nicky was self-compassion cultivation. They embarked on a profound shift in mindset, starting by treating themselves with kindness and understanding. Acknowledging that jealousy is a natural emotion, they reframed their perception, recognising that it did not define their worth. Through introspection and reflection, they delved deeper, uncovering the underlying insecurities and fears that fuelled their jealousy. This process of self-discovery allowed them to develop a heightened sense of self-awareness. Armed with this newfound understanding, we consciously practised self-compassion, challenging the self-critical inner dialogue that had plagued them. Ronaldo and Nicky replaced this dialogue with supportive words and thoughts, creating a nurturing environment and applying the three-brain equilibrium method (Chapter 4). This practice fostered acceptance and love for who they are, free from the constraints of comparison and jealousy—by embracing self-compassion.

Effectively managing anxiety is central to your drive to overcome jealousy. You can recognise that anxiety often fuels your jealousy and hinders your well-being, and learn to challenge your anxious thoughts and develop a more balanced mindset by employing cognitive restructuring and reframing techniques. Replacing your anxious thoughts with rational and empowering ones creates space for more positive emotions and constructive actions. This proactive approach to managing anxiety will enable you to approach jealousy with clarity, resilience, and a healthier perspective. This highlights the power of self-growth, self-compassion, and anxiety management in navigating and overcoming jealousy, empowering you to support your authentic self and live a more fulfilling life.

Finally, let's delve into the most intriguing case Lily and her partner, Gary. Lily's journey as a transgender woman provides a unique and fascinating perspective on jealousy. Despite her popularity on social media and finding love with Gary, a heterosexual male partner, she struggled with insecurities and occasional bouts of jealousy triggered by her partner's interactions with other females. These challenges required careful navigation to address the underlying causes and foster a healthy and secure relationship. As I worked with the couple, I found that Lily's feelings of insecurity and jealousy stemmed from a combination of factors influenced by her experiences as a transgender individual. First, her own journey of self-acceptance and transitioning exposed her to societal pressures and expectations surrounding femininity, beauty, and desirability, contributing to her feelings of inadequacy. Additionally, Gary's interactions with other females made her question her attractiveness and femininity compared to cisgender women. Her biggest fear was rejection because of her past issues around her self-acceptance.

Open and honest communication became paramount for Lily and Gary to address these challenges. Creating a safe and non-judgemental space allowed them to candidly discuss their insecurities, fears, and expectations, fostering trust and emotional security within their relationship. In addition, Gary played a crucial role in nurturing their connection by expressing unwavering commitment and support, assuring her that their connection was based on a deep emotional bond rather than solely external appearances.

Simultaneously, Lily embarked on a journey of self-esteem building and self-acceptance. Engaging in activities promoting self-care, self-expression, and self-love allowed her to cultivate confidence and resilience. In addition, seeking support from the transgender community or therapy provided valuable guidance and empowerment as she embraced her authentic self. As she did so, her relationship improved as the fear of rejection subsided.

Understanding the underlying dynamics of jealousy and the detrimental impact of comparisonitis is essential. Anxiety fuels the constant need for validation through comparison, perpetuating feelings of inadequacy and jealousy. By consciously challenging anxious thought patterns, you can break free from the suffocating grip of comparisonitis, redirect your focus towards personal growth and fulfilment, and encourage self-acceptance.

Fostering healthy relationships requires open communication, empathy, and trust in the face of jealousy. By embracing self-acceptance, nurturing resilience, and rejecting the destructive cycle of comparison, you can transcend the limitations of jealousy and create authentic connections based on mutual understanding.

Unravelling the intricacies of jealousy and comparisonitis will set you on a positive journey towards change, self-acceptance, emotional well-being, and healthier relationships. This journey begins by acknowledging each person's unique path and embracing self-consideration, enabling personal growth and liberation from anxiety. Next, understanding the complexities of these emotions involves exploring diverse scenarios and the interplay of fear, comparisonitis, and jealousy. Finally, self-reflection and practising mindfulness will allow you to pause, empathise, and reframe your internal dialogues, fostering healthier perspectives in your interactions.

It is vital to recognise the immense power of words, particularly when it comes to jealousy. Unfortunately, people experiencing this emotion often find themselves trapped in a cycle of intense negativity, leading to self-destructive, self-sabotaging thoughts, sights, and expressions of hate towards themselves and others. However, it is crucial to understand that feeling jealous does not make you inherently bad. Instead, it is essential to shift away from unproductive thinking patterns and focus on fostering healthier relationships and communication dynamics.

Critical Self-Perception

Anxiety, an everyday companion of jealousy, intensifies your critical self-perception. It creates a steady inner voice that seldom listens to others, particularly when they express positivity. This harsh inner critic erodes self-esteem, fuelled by negative belief systems and self-imposed labels. As a therapist, I have witnessed how negative thinking patterns and self-talk make people clingy seeking constant reassurance from their friends, colleagues, family, and partners. Worry, overthinking, suspicion, jealousy, and other insecure emotions permeate their relationships in the absence of partners. Looking back at Lily's case, she felt her insecurities and needed validation and security from her partner and audience. The overwhelming flood of questions and paranoia engulfed her thoughts, driving self-sabotage, self-doubt, and insecurity. As a result, she turned against herself first and then directed her insecurities towards her partner and those surrounding her. This cascade of anxiety-driven thoughts, emotions, and beliefs manifested as severe reactions, leading to jealousy, anger, and resentment. Unfortunately, this behaviour can persist across all relationships, resulting in a cycle of hurtful reactions, criticism, anger, and withdrawal. The person on the receiving end of these responses can then react with what the jealous partner most fears rejection.

However, there are strategies to break free from this pattern. Repairing relationships, both with yourself and others, is a vital step. Recognising that all emotions excluding extremely harmful tendencies—are normal allows you to approach them rationally. Stepping back, pausing, and thinking before reacting, and calmly responding instead, helps maintain rational thoughts and allows for effective communication. Prioritising self-care supports your overall well-being and enhances your ability to navigate jealousy and anxiety-related relationship issues.

Interestingly, when delving into jealousy, it is essential to recognise the prevailing sense of caution that often surrounds it. Within Indian Asian culture, envy carries particular significance due to the deeply ingrained belief in the "evil eye", known as *Nazar*. This cultural backdrop adds a unique dimension as individuals navigate their lives with a mindful awareness of potential jealousy and the fear of attracting negativity through the evil eye.

The notion of the evil eye, or Nazar, is deeply rooted in the belief that intense jealousy or envy from others can cast a malevolent gaze upon an individual, causing harm or misfortune. This belief reflects the psychological aspects of jealousy, intertwining it with the power of perception and the potential influence of others' negative emotions. Furthermore, it highlights the fears and anxieties associated with personal successes, as individuals may hesitate to share or celebrate their achievements out of concern for attracting jealousy and the resulting adverse effects.

From a psychological standpoint, the concept of Nazar reflects the impact of social comparison and its role in jealousy. Social comparison theory suggests that individuals naturally assess themselves concerning others, often leading to envy or inferiority when perceiving others as more successful or fortunate. In the context of Nazar, this comparison can be heightened by the cultural belief in the malevolent gaze of jealousy.

The psychological implications of Nazar extend beyond individual well-being to interpersonal relationships. This dynamic can create a climate of secrecy and inhibition, hindering open communication and genuine celebration of one another's achievements. The belief in the evil eye and its influence on jealousy provides insights into the complexities of human psychology, transcending cultural boundaries. Jealousy, rooted in feelings of insecurity and comparison, evokes a range of psychological responses that impact personal well-being and relationships.

I know all too well from the many people I have worked with, as well as from my own experience, that unhealthy comparisons exacerbate these effects, hindering personal growth. However, approaching comparisons with self-awareness allows for positive change and introspection. Appreciating others' accomplishments becomes a source of motivation, nurturing a deeper appreciation of your own strengths. Through self-acceptance and gratitude, you can navigate life's challenges, liberating yourself from the burden of comparison with others, striving to reflect on who you are, and embracing who you will become.

In any journey of personal growth and self-discovery, healthy competition will propel you beyond limitations, while honouring the uniqueness of your own path. Through graceful navigation of life's intricacies, you will embrace authenticity. The radiant light of harmony and self-fulfilment will illuminate your existence, creating a harmonious coexistence with others.

Fix Me Tools

Embrace Laughter Therapy. Incorporate the power of laughter into your life. Engage in activities that make you laugh, such as watching comedies, sharing jokes with friends, or participating in laughter yoga exercises. Laughter can help alleviate tension, shift perspective, and reduce anxiety, including jealousy. Find moments of joy and humour to lighten your emotional load.

Reflect on Self-Worth. Explore jealousy's underlying causes by examining your feelings of self-worth. Recognise that jealousy often stems from insecurities and a lack of self-acceptance. Work on building self-esteem and embracing your unique qualities and strengths. Practice self-love and self-care and surround yourself with positive affirmations and supportive people.

Address the Root Cause. Dig deeper into the root cause of your jealousy. Ask yourself what you feel bad about and what's fuelling your anxious thoughts. Understanding the underlying issues can help you have meaningful conversations with yourself, leading to personal growth and reduced jealousy. Challenge negative beliefs and replace them with more empowering and self-affirming thoughts and words.

Nurture Self-Care. Prioritise self-care activities that promote relaxation and well-being. Engage in activities that bring you joy and happiness and do what you love. Whether pursuing hobbies, spending time in nature, practising self-compassion, or engaging in creative outlets, prioritise self-care. Taking care of yourself emotionally, mentally, and physically will enhance your overall well-being and help diminish feelings of jealousy.

Cultivate Trust. Focus on building trust within yourself. Trust your instincts, honour your boundaries, and make decisions that align with your values. Develop self-trust by being reliable and accountable to yourself. Build a strong foundation of self-trust, which will positively impact your relationships and reduce feelings of jealousy.

In this chapter, we have explored the complex relationship between jealousy and anxiety, and witnessed how self-reflection, self-compassion, and therapy can help overcome jealousy. By managing your anxiety, practising self-care, and cultivating self-worth, you can break free from the cycle of jealousy. The cultural significance of jealousy and the belief in the evil eye were discussed, emphasising the importance of self-awareness and the impact of social comparison. By embracing laughter therapy, nurturing your self-worth, and fostering self-acceptance, you can navigate jealousy, find inner healing, and ultimately experience peace in your life.

10

Self-Relationship Anxiety

....

Reflecting on the last chapter, we delved into the intricate relationship between jealousy and anxiety, exploring their profound impact on your emotional well-being and personal growth. We uncovered the detrimental effects of anxiety-driven comparison and the distortions it can create in your perceptions. As we transition into this chapter, we will focus on self-relationships and how anxiety can profoundly influence your connection with others.

This chapter will delve into the concept of self-relationships and explore how anxiety influences our connection with ourselves and others. Self-relationships encompass how we perceive, interact with, and care for ourselves. Anxiety can significantly impact this internal dynamic, leading to feelings of insecurity, mistrust, and vulnerability. These emotions often extend into our relationships with others, affecting our ability to establish deep and meaningful connections.

By understanding the manifestations of anxiety within our self-relationships, we gain valuable insights into the potential hindrances in forming authentic connections with others. Moreover, examining these dynamics helps us identify thought and behaviour patterns contributing to relationship challenges. With this awareness, we can employ effective strategies and practices to navigate our relationships with ease, authenticity, and emotional well-being.

Recognising the interplay between your self-relationship and your relationships with others is crucial. Cultivating a healthy self-relationship positively influences your interactions with others, while challenges in your relationships can impact your self-perception and overall well-being. Addressing anxiety within your self-relationship establishes a solid foundation for fostering fulfilling connections with others. This chapter provides valuable insights, tools, and techniques to nurture your self-relationships, enhance your ability to form meaningful connections, and project a positive reflection in your relationships.

In your life, relationships play a vital role in shaping your experiences and contributing to your happiness. Addressing and managing anxiety within the context of your connections can pave the way for healthier and more enriching relationships. Let's explore the intricate interplay between anxiety and self-relationships, discovering pathways towards fostering greater understanding, development, and confidence.

No one starts a relationship to end it, but sadly, many relationships break down because people struggle to understand, heal, or find confidence in themselves. As a social being, it's natural for you to long for love and seek affection from family, friends, and romantic partners. However, it's essential not to overlook your most important relationship with yourself while pursuing external validation.

It's common to wonder why you struggle to find someone who loves you as deeply as you love them. The truth may lie in the power of genuine self-love, which enhances your relationships and helps you manage anxiety more effectively. Unfortunately, authentic self-love is often overlooked and undervalued in our society. It goes beyond surface-level acts of self-care and involves developing a profound appreciation for your own company. I always tell my clients that if you want to accept the truth about yourself, you've got to embrace the good, the bad, and the ugly aspects. This means embracing your strengths, acknowledging your weaknesses, and treating yourself kindly.

Embarking on self-love can be challenging, requiring introspection, vulnerability, and a willingness to confront your innermost fears and insecurities. Unfortunately, societal conditioning often leads you to seek external validation and perceive self-love as selfish or indulgent. As a result, you may struggle to prioritise your needs and find it difficult to accept and love yourself fully.

Developing a strong sense of self-love can help you break free from co-dependency patterns, which can harm both parties involved. Co-dependency arises from a lack of self-love, where one person becomes overly dependent on another for emotional and psychological needs, leading to a loss of autonomy, self-esteem, and self-worth. When you learn to love yourself, you can develop a healthy sense of independence. In addition, you can build healthy relationships based on mutual respect and trust, without relying solely on others for validation.

This shift in perspective reduces the anxiety that arises from seeking approval from others, allowing you to become more self-reliant and resilient. By learning to love yourself, you can break free from patterns of co-dependency, fostering healthier relationships and promoting personal growth and well-being. The profound concept of self-regard is at the core of building a healthy relationship with yourself. Self-love encompasses the development of high self-worth, self-confidence, and self-efficacy, which are critical in establishing clear boundaries and effective communication in your relationships.

When you nurture self-regard, you are more likely to attract partners who value and respect you for who you truly are, rather than settling for less or seeking constant support from others. The association between self-love and secure attachment styles underscores the essential nature of self-regard in developing healthy relationships. Those with secure attachment styles exhibit well-defined boundaries, confidently communicate their needs, and possess a strong sense of self-worth, trust, and independence. As a result, they can enter relationships authentically and wholeheartedly, fostering deeper connections based on mutual respect, love, and support.

In contrast, people with insecure attachment styles may find it challenging to establish healthy boundaries and express their needs, leading to co-dependency patterns in their relationships. However, by adopting a solid foundation of self-love, you can transcend these attachment patterns and develop healthier relationships, experiencing a deep sense of satisfaction and empowerment in your interpersonal connections.

Know Who You Are

In my encounters with numerous individuals, including my personal experiences, I have observed a tendency to give excessively to others regarding love, time, and abilities. However, as the pilot on a flight advises, put the oxygen mask on yourself first. You must attend to yourself before attending to others. I will use this analogy to emphasise the importance of prioritising your own well-being, as only by doing so can you genuinely help those around you. Yet, as we embark on the expedition of self-healing and self-love, perhaps, like me, you often have to contend with the insidious presence of imposter syndrome an all-encompassing phenomenon that erodes self-confidence and obstructs the recognition of your own capabilities.

Despite outward displays of confidence, I spent many years battling with inner doubts and perceiving myself as fraudulent, undeserving, and, for some reason, felt that I would be found out. Well, of course, I am revealing all in this book. But I figured that my issue was because of money. People assume entrepreneurs are rolling in money; most are. My parents were small business owners, and I grew up with that same mindset. I was always the one that worked harder in class to get validated. The one who didn't do particularly well at school. The one who worked two jobs after school and on the weekends. The one who struggled. Thankfully, I let that all go. Nevertheless, by embracing the essential practice of self-love and acknowledging that I deserve my achievements, I was able to courageously confront imposter syndrome, wholeheartedly accepting my unique talents with authenticity and unwavering confidence. The secret formula, if there is one, is to stop judging yourself, then you will not fear the judgement of others.

Let me share the story of a client, Steve, whom I empathise with deeply. Steve struggled with performance anxiety as a speaker and battled imposter syndrome. Despite his immense talents and numerous accomplishments, he constantly doubted his abilities, fearing that he would be exposed as a fraud. This anxiety had a significant impact on his performance at speaking events. Steve's concerns stemmed from a deeply ingrained belief that he was unworthy of his achievements. Despite his remarkable success as a businessperson, his upbringing on a council estate in East London left him feeling like an imposter, questioning whether he truly deserved the good things in his life. This sense of indebtedness and the weight of his past drove him to set unrealistic standards, intensifying his self-doubt. This internal narrative of inadequacy fuelled his anxiety, hindering his ability to fully embrace his inherent potential and celebrate his accomplishments, particularly now that he lives a luxurious life in Los Angeles.

To help Steve, we worked on improving his self-acceptance and self-compassion. He learnt to be vulnerable, appreciate his unique strengths, and recognise his accomplishments as genuine reflections of his abilities. We reflected on the past, discussing what made him feel determined to be successful in the first place. We went back to when he felt ambitious to move away from what he described as his rut and "soiled environment". Over time, he progressed further, enhanced by implementing cognitive and mindfulness techniques. As Steve's therapist, I worked with him to challenge his negative self-talk and replace it with positive affirmations. Additionally, I created a personalised meditative recording that focused on his unique capabilities, intended to reach his subconscious mind while in an alpha state. This technique is supported by the work of Bruce Lipton, a renowned cellular biologist, who explains that the subconscious mind plays a critical role in shaping our beliefs and behaviours (Lipton, 2015).

In his book, Lipton explains how our subconscious mind controls up to 95% of our thoughts, emotions, and behaviours, shaping our self-perception and worldview. By accessing the power of the subconscious mind through meditation and hypnosis, you can reprogram your beliefs and perceptions, leading to more positive thoughts and behaviours. You can overcome performance anxiety and imposter syndrome through personalised meditative recordings and other techniques, unlocking your full potential and experiencing greater well-being. As we delved into Steve's perspective of his younger self and the hunger he had to succeed, we fostered a compassionate and empowering view, gradually shifting his mindset and embracing his true capabilities.

As Steve's journey towards overcoming performance anxiety and imposter syndrome unfolded, he underwent a profound transformation in his self-perception. Through a conscious reflection of self-love and self-compassion, Steve shifted his mindset from a perfection-oriented perspective to a growth-oriented one, embracing his mistakes and using them as opportunities for learning and growth. With this newfound self-acceptance, Steve was empowered to recognise that his worth was not tied to external validation or approval, but rather came from within himself. This realisation allowed him to approach challenges with greater confidence, take risks, and focus on his own growth and self-improvement, by becoming a mentor to his younger self, guiding and navigating him on a route to success, ultimately leading to greater well-being and mental health. Ultimately Steve learnt to improve, by not comparing himself to others, but only to the person he used to be.

Steve's journey is a testament to the profound impact of self-compassion, inspiring individuals in various walks of life. Whether in the public eye or leading ordinary lives, we often find ourselves trapped in a cycle of self-judgement, constantly comparing ourselves to others and scrutinising our own flaws and shortcomings. In these moments, the practice of self-love becomes even more crucial.

In the case of another client, Mike, his story highlights the devastating consequences of self-judgement manifested in body dysmorphic disorder (BDD). Mike was hyperaware of his weight and appearance, consistently measuring himself against societal standards and feeling dissatisfied with his body. His self-judgement persisted, despite reassurances from loved ones, resulting in significant distress and a diminished sense of self-worth.

BDD is a mental health condition characterised by an obsessive preoccupation with perceived flaws or defects in one's appearance. Individuals with BDD experience intense distress and engage in repetitive behaviours or rituals to conceal or correct these imperfections. In Mike's case, his obsession with his weight and appearance consumed his thoughts, leading to anxiety, depression, and a profound erosion of his self-esteem.

Comparing Mike's experience to Steve's journey, we witness the contrasting outcomes that self-judgement and self-love can produce in individuals' lives. Steve's story exemplifies the transformative power of self-love, enabling him to navigate personal challenges, embrace his inherent worthiness, and cultivate a positive mindset. In contrast, Mike's struggle with BDD showcases the detrimental effects of self-judgement on mental well-being and self-perception.

Through self-judgement, Mike perpetuated a destructive cycle of negative thoughts and emotions, reinforcing his dissatisfaction with his appearance. Conversely, Steve's journey demonstrated the practice of self-love, allowing him to nurture a compassionate and accepting relationship with himself, leading to improved self-esteem and well-being. This distinction emphasises the significant impact of self-perception and self-compassion on mental health and overall quality of life.

Overcoming self-judgement and fostering self-regard is a complex and non-linear process that often necessitates professional support, such as therapy or counselling. Mike sought therapeutic intervention, gradually challenging his self-judgement and humanising self-acceptance and self-compassion. Through treatment, Mike learned to shift his focus from external appearance to inner qualities and strengths, letting go of unrealistic expectations and embracing his unique beauty. Listen to your body's needs. Tune in to your body's signals and respond to its needs. For example, Mike started to pay attention to hunger and fullness cues, eating mindfully and permitting himself to enjoy foods without guilt or restriction by honouring his body's need for movement, rest, and relaxation. This shift in mindset positively influenced his self-esteem, well-being, and interpersonal relationships.

Celebrate Who You Are

By treating yourself with the same admiration and unconditional love you bestow upon your favourite people or celebrities, you will shift your perspective and affirm your intrinsic worthiness. Self-love involves celebrating your accomplishments, acknowledging your progress, and practising self-compassion. It's about being kind to yourself, caring for your holistic well-being during challenging times, and recognising your shared humanity and inherent fallibility.

Whether in the public eye or leading an ordinary life, you deserve moments of self-love and self-care. It's not an act of arrogance but a recognition of your inherent value and the importance of prioritising your well-being. By nurturing self-love, you nourish your mind, body, and soul, establishing a foundation of self-acceptance and resilience that positively impacts every aspect of your life.

When you choose self-love, you liberate yourself from self-judgement and support a kinder and more compassionate inner dialogue. This shift in mindset influences how you perceive yourself and interact with others. It releases good hormones. It empowers you to show up authentically and confidently, free from the constraints of comparison and self-doubt. By embracing self-love, you recognise your inherent worthiness and realise that you are lovable, good enough, and deserving of all life's goodness. And with all those chemical releases that make you feel fabulous and impressive, you can nurture a deep sense of empathy and kindness towards yourself, which naturally extends to how you treat and interact with others. This is then mirrored back to you. So, remember, treat yourself the way you expect others to.

Just as Steve's journey exemplified the profound power of self-regard, Mike's story showcases the potential for healing and growth when we prioritise our well-being. While their experiences differed, both individuals confronted the destructive nature of self-judgement and discovered the profound impact that self-love could have on their lives.

In summary, nurturing self-love and self-compassion is a lifelong practice that requires patience, self-reflection, and the willingness to challenge negative beliefs and patterns. It is about recognising your worthiness, embracing your imperfections, and treating yourself with the same kindness and understanding you would extend to your loved ones. By cultivating self-love, you create a foundation of strength and resilience that empowers you to navigate life's challenges with grace and authenticity. It is a powerful journey of self-discovery that allows you to embrace your true selves, unleash your potential, and lead lives filled with joy and deep connection.

Fix Me Tools

Look in the Mirror. Stand in front of a mirror and look into your own eyes. Speak affirmations such as "I am worthy of love and respect". . . " I embrace my unique qualities". . . or "I am enough just as I am." Notice your reflection and observe how these positive statements resonate within you. For example, you might say "I appreciate the kindness I show to others" or "I admire my ability to overcome challenges with resilience." Mirror work helps to build a deeper connection with yourself and reinforce self-love through visual and verbal affirmation.

Practice Ho'oponopono. Ho'oponopono is a traditional Hawaiian practice of reconciliation and forgiveness. It is a spiritual and healing technique that aims to restore harmony within oneself and with others. The method involves taking responsibility for one's experiences and offering forgiveness and love to oneself and others. I have practised this for many years, especially during those dark and turbulent times. To embrace the principles of Ho'oponopono, repeat the mantra "I'm sorry, please forgive me, thank you, I love you." Use this mantra to heal past wounds, release resentment, and cultivate forgiveness. For instance, you can say "I'm sorry for any pain I may have caused myself or others. Please forgive me for holding onto negative emotions. Thank you for the opportunity to heal and grow. I love myself unconditionally." Practice this mantra regularly, either silently or out loud, allowing it to bring about a sense of peace, healing, and self-acceptance (Vitale and Len, 2008).

Keep a Gratitude Journal. Dedicate a journal specifically for gratitude. When you get a chance, either in the morning or last thing at night, write down three things you are grateful for. These can be simple pleasures, moments of joy, acts of kindness, or personal achievements. For example, you might express gratitude for a supportive friend, a beautiful sunset, or your own perseverance in overcoming a challenge. As you consistently engage in gratitude journalling, you will develop a positive mindset and a greater gratitude for yourself and the world around you.

Prioritise Self-Care Rituals. Develop personalised self-care rituals that nourish your emotional, mental, and physical well-being. This might involve creating a peaceful morning routine with meditation or walking, treating yourself to a spa day at home with a bubble bath and scented candles, or engaging in a hobby or activity that brings you delight and relaxation. For instance, you could set aside time each week for a nature walk, to practice yoga, paint, sing, or engage in creative writing. Prioritising self-care communicates self-love and strengthens your relationship with yourself.

Use Affirmations and Mantras. Create your own affirmations and mantras that resonate with your self-love journey. Tailor them to address areas where you may struggle or seek improvement. For example, if you are working on self-acceptance, affirmations such as "I embrace my flaws and celebrate my uniqueness" or "I am worthy of love and acceptance exactly as I am" can be empowering. Repeat these affirmations daily, silently or aloud, and believe in their truth to reprogram your subconscious mind and strengthen self-love.

Surround Yourself with Positivity. This is the one many people have complained to me about. They say what if we can't choose the people, such as family, around us? Well, I agree you can't occasionally, but if you cannot remove yourself from them, change how you respond to them. Evaluate the people, environments, and media you expose yourself to. And with the things you can control, surround yourself with individuals who uplift and support you, create a home environment that reflects your values and brings you joy, and curate your social media feed to include accounts that promote self-love, personal growth, and positivity. For example, follow inspirational speakers, read books that inspire self-empowerment, and engage in communities or groups that foster a sense of belonging and encouragement.

Set Healthy Boundaries. Establishing healthy boundaries is an act of self-love. Identify areas in your life where you may be overextending yourself or allowing others to take advantage of your time and energy. Learn to say no when necessary and communicate your needs and limits clearly and assertively. By setting and maintaining healthy boundaries, you create space for self-care, prioritise your well-being, and honour your own needs, fostering self-love and self-respect.

Engage in Self-Reflection and Self-Discovery. Dedicate time for self-reflection and self-discovery. Engage in practices that help you better understand yourself and cultivate self-love. This can involve exploring your thoughts, emotions, and desires. Reflect on your values, passions, and strengths. Ask yourself meaningful questions like "What brings me joy?" or "What are my core beliefs?" Self-reflection allows you to clarify who you are and what matters most to you, nurturing a more profound sense of self-love.

Celebrate Your Achievements. Acknowledge and celebrate your accomplishments, big and small. Create rituals or reward systems to commemorate milestones and successes. This can be as simple as treating yourself to a special meal, buying a small gift, or writing a congratulatory letter. Recognising and celebrating your achievements reinforces a positive self-image, builds confidence, and strengthens self-love.

Focus on Positive Self-Talk. Focus on your inner dialogue and challenge negative self-talk. Replace self-criticism with kind and compassionate self-talk. Whenever you notice negative thoughts or self-doubt, consciously shift your perspective to focus on your strengths, achievements, and positive attributes. Practice affirmations that affirm your self-worth and remind yourself that you deserve love and kindness. Positive self-talk nurtures self-love and empowers you to embrace your authentic self.

Remember, self-love is an ongoing journey that requires patience and consistent effort. Experiment with different tools and techniques to discover what resonates with you. Be gentle with yourself and allow for self-discovery and progress along the way. By investing in self-love, you will cultivate a deep sense of worthiness and well-being, enabling you to live a flourishing and serene life.

References

Lipton, B. (2016). *The Biology of Belief.* Carlsbad, CA: Hay House.
Vitale, J. and Len, I. H. (2008). *Zero Limits: The Secret Hawaiian System for Wealth, Health, Peace, and More.* New York: Wiley.

11

Managing Social Anxiety

....

In the previous chapter, we delved deeply into self-relationships, addressing the barriers that hinder personal growth and emphasising the significance of self-compassion and self-acceptance. Building upon those invaluable insights, our focus now turns to a pressing issue that plagues many individuals in the modern world: social anxiety.

Social anxiety has become increasingly prevalent, particularly with the global COVID-19 pandemic and the subsequent decrease in face-to-face interactions. Activities that were once effortless now have the power to trigger anxiety, underscoring the significant impact social anxiety can have on our well-being and daily lives.

This chapter aims to explore the intricacies of social anxiety, uncover its underlying causes, and provide practical approaches for managing and overcoming it. Recognising that everyone's experiences are unique, I aim to empower individuals with diverse strategies to navigate social anxiety on their own terms.

Developing a support network of understanding friends, family, or support groups is crucial. Connecting with others who empathise with our struggles provides validation, support, and valuable coping strategies. We will also explore various techniques for managing social anxiety, including relaxation exercises, mindfulness practices, assertiveness training, and gradual exposure to social situations in a controlled and supportive manner.

Highlighting self-care is integral to our exploration of social anxiety. Participating in activities that promote overall well-being such as exercise, maintaining a healthy lifestyle, and practising self-nurturing routines—can significantly help manage social anxiety symptoms. Prioritising self-care establishes a foundation for resilience and fosters a positive self-relationship, as mentioned in previous chapters.

The main goal of this chapter is to provide you with a wide range of tools and insights that will help you effectively manage social anxiety keeping in mind and respecting that everyone's experiences and needs are unique. Therefore, I encourage you to explore and experiment to discover strategies that authentically resonate with you. By developing these skills and enriching resilience, you will be able to navigate social situations with a newfound sense of confidence and ease.

Before delving further, let's examine the distinction between social anxiety and agoraphobia. Social anxiety disorder, also sometimes known as *social phobia*, involves an intense fear and anxiety in social situations where individuals may face scrutiny, judgement, or potential embarrassment. The fear of negative evaluation and the desire to avoid social interactions or endure them with distress are central features of social anxiety. On the other hand, *agoraphobia* is characterised by a fear of being in places or situations where escape may be difficult, or help may not readily be available during a panic attack or anxiety episode. This fear often leads individuals to avoid crowded places, public transportation, open spaces, or leaving their homes altogether.

While both social anxiety disorder and agoraphobia involve anxiety and avoidance behaviours, the distinction lies in the specific triggering situations. Social anxiety disorder is characterised by the fear of negative evaluation in social interactions, while agoraphobia centres around the fear of being trapped in challenging situations. For instance, individuals with social anxiety may experience intense apprehension before attending a social gathering, dreading the possibility of saying something wrong or being judged by others. This fear can lead them to withdraw and avoid active participation in conversations or events. On the other hand, someone with agoraphobia may find themselves overwhelmed by anxiety at the mere thought of taking public transportation. They may feel trapped and limited in their ability to explore new places or engage in activities outside their immediate surroundings, often opting to avoid such situations altogether. It's important to note that individuals can experience both social anxiety disorder and agoraphobia concurrently or separately. Professional diagnosis and treatment are essential for accurate assessment and appropriate management of these conditions, and the tools are there to help you cope.

Fear of Social Situations

As a therapist, I recognise the immense value of providing unwavering support and understanding to individuals navigating the intricate terrain of social anxiety disorder. One such individual is Bob, who experienced debilitating panic attacks whenever he ventured out into social settings. He used to feel an overwhelming sense of unease and fear, convinced that he would be scrutinised or judged by others. These panic attacks left him feeling trapped and helpless, leading him to isolate himself and avoid social interactions altogether. That's how bad social anxiety can hit someone; they can be overwhelmed with panic and then spiral into a state of complete fear. Through our therapeutic exploration together, I created a safe and non-judgemental space for Bob to explore the underlying causes of his anxiety and develop effective coping strategies.

For instance, at the beginning of our therapeutic journey, Bob held a strong belief that people would judge him harshly in social settings. However, as we explored his experiences and emotions, we uncovered a complex web of underlying factors that contributed to his panic attacks. We discovered that his fear of rejection and lack of self-confidence stemmed from a significant childhood experience. Bob had a skin condition during his early years that resulted in other children avoiding him and rejecting his attempts to engage in play. They would bully him, and he would fear going to school (bullying is covered in Chapter 12). This deeply ingrained fear of rejection became a trigger for his social anxiety.

By bringing awareness to this pivotal experience and its lingering impact, we were able to address the core issues and work on building his self-confidence. During our therapeutic journey, we utilised various techniques to support Bob in managing his social anxiety. One technique that proved beneficial was progressive muscle relaxation. This approach involves systematically tensing and then releasing different muscle groups in the body, promoting deep physical relaxation and reducing overall tension. By guiding Bob through this relaxation exercise, he was able to learn how to recognise and release muscle tension associated with the anxiety. This technique provided him with a tangible tool to use in moments of heightened stress, helping him to calm his body and mind, and promoting a sense of relaxation and control. Bob gradually developed strategies to challenge his fears, reframe his negative beliefs, and help him be more positive and resilient. As we discovered what triggered his fear, he slowly let go with each muscle relaxation exercise he did, and learned mostly to do this on his own. Over time, he began to navigate social interactions with greater ease and assurance, finding a renewed sense of self-worth and genuine connections with others.

Lee, another client of mine, contended with extreme self-consciousness while walking down the street. He lacked confidence in initiating greetings and would respond meekly when compelled to do so. Lee went to great lengths to hide his worries, avoiding eye contact and silently repeating a mantra, desperately hoping to make it home without interacting with anyone. Over time, this avoidance and anxiety became his daily routine. However, Lee's story took a distressing turn when he abruptly stopped attending our sessions. After several weeks, he reached out to inform me that he had been hit by a car and had broken his leg. The incident occurred when he panicked upon seeing his neighbour and crossed the road without looking, consumed by fear. This unfortunate event served as a painful reminder of the physical harm that can result from unaddressed social anxiety.

Social anxiety, with its complicated indicators, unveils a lot of fears and uncertainties that grip individuals in the realm of social interactions. The fear of being judged or assessed by others, coupled with a pervasive uncertainty over how to navigate social situations, paints a vivid portrait of the internal struggle many people face. Worries about visible signs of anxiety, such as sweaty palms or stumbling over words, further compound the distress. To truly address and effectively manage social anxiety, it is paramount to delve beneath the surface, peeling back the layers to uncover the root causes that give rise to this intricate web of fear. By delving into the thoughts, feelings, and patterns of behaviour entwined with social anxiety, individuals can gain valuable insights into its origin and the profound pain it inflicts. This recognition forms the bedrock for seeking and implementing strategies that can alleviate the impact of social anxiety and restore a sense of balance and confidence in the realm of social interactions.

Confinement and Escape

Whereas agoraphobia is characterised by a fear of being in situations where escape may be challenging, it can often feel more tangible and straightforward to address. This is because agoraphobia involves specific triggers and scenarios that individuals can identify and work on gradually. A poignant example is that of my client, Christina, who struggled with agoraphobia. She experienced intense anxiety when in crowded places or confined spaces, often avoiding them altogether. However, through our therapeutic journey, Christina learned to face her fears by gradually exposing herself to these situations in a controlled and supportive manner. She practised relaxation techniques to manage her anxiety and utilised cognitive-behavioural strategies, such as reframing negative thoughts and challenging catastrophic thinking patterns. We challenged and examined these thoughts and reviewed her coping mechanisms, gathering evidence, considering alternative perspectives, and developing more balanced and rational thinking patterns. For instance, we challenged Christina's beliefs. She thought she would get squashed, stop breathing, and suffocate to death. By exploring evidence of positive past social interactions, considering alternative explanations for others' behaviours, and reframing her thoughts about the reality of a situation, Christina's basic fear was the discomfort she felt about other people's body odour or people being too close to her. Over time, she slowly explored places that were not confined; she would go with a trusted friend if she thought there were fewer than expected people. As she explored her emotions, she realised that she feared getting ill from other people if they were too close by her. She used to think she would get an illness, and this was even before the pandemic hit; it only got worse then. It took time, but slowly she regained a sense of freedom and empowerment to move away from situations that made her feel restrained.

Similarly, I personally experienced a form of agoraphobia during my time working in London. The bustling and crowded environment of the tube became a source of overwhelming stress and discomfort for me. After a long day at work, I would impatiently squeeze into a packed train carriage, desperately wanting to reach home quickly. However, I soon realised that this approach only fuelled my anxiety further. I learned the importance of patience and self-care in managing my agoraphobia. If I felt overwhelmed, I would purposefully wait for a less crowded train or find a space away from the situation, and sometimes even travel a longer journey on a bus that was less crowded. For me, it was working out other means to accommodate my needs. And this is important, which brings me back to what I said before: we must be self-aware of our needs and once we accept a situation, we can give ourselves the self-compassion we need. This shift in mindset and behaviour helped me navigate the challenges of public transportation with greater ease and reduced the anxiety, because I found what worked for me. A crucial aspect of social anxiety treatment involves the management of anticipatory anxiety. Anticipatory anxiety refers to the fear and worry experienced before social situations or events, where individuals may anticipate negative evaluation or judgement from others. This entails identifying triggers that elicit fear and gradually exposing oneself to these feared social situations, fostering resilience and tolerance over time. By gradually facing and overcoming these anxieties, individuals with social anxiety can develop increased confidence and reduce the intensity of anticipatory anxiety. Another valuable technique is scheduling designated "worry time", which provides a structured opportunity to address anxieties and concerns. During this dedicated period, individuals can focus on their worries, actively address them, and explore potential solutions. This practice allows for a sense of containment and control over anxiety-inducing thoughts. This will help people be present and focus on what is happening around them rather than getting distracted by the overwhelming idea of worry. Additionally, cognitive-behavioural techniques such as challenging irrational thoughts and engaging in relaxation exercises reduce anxiety symptoms and promote a greater sense of personal agency. By integrating these strategies into the treatment plan, individuals with social anxiety or agoraphobia can develop effective coping mechanisms, gradually confront their fears, and encourage a renewed sense of confidence and empowerment.

By sharing the case examples of individuals like Bob, Lee, and Christina, we shed light on the profound significance of acknowledging and addressing social anxiety and agoraphobia. Through dedicated self-therapeutic and therapy interventions and targeted strategies, these individuals gradually conquered their fears, reclaimed control over their lives, and navigated social situations with renewed confidence and resilience.

Knowing When You Need Help

Understanding the distinction between social anxiety and normal shyness or nervousness, as well as performance anxiety or public speaking concerns, is of paramount importance. While it is common to experience self-consciousness in unfamiliar social settings, or feel a level of nervousness when speaking in public, it is crucial to recognise that social anxiety becomes a more significant concern when it is overwhelming, profoundly impacts daily life, or leads to avoidance of specific situations or activities. The cases of Bob, Lee and Christina exemplify how anxiety can gradually shape and constrain your life, underscoring the necessity of seeking appropriate support and interventions to address the underlying social anxiety. By differentiating social anxiety from transient feelings of shyness or performance-related nerves, you can discern the need for professional help and embark on a transformative path towards healing and personal growth.

Through self-therapy and professional guidance, individuals like Bob, Lee, and Christina embarked on a profound journey towards healing and growth. They acquired effective coping mechanisms, challenged negative thought patterns, and gradually confronted their fears in a supportive and controlled manner. This process empowered them to reclaim their power, break free from the limitations of anxiety, and cultivate a greater sense of self-assurance and overall well-being. By acknowledging and addressing your fears, and focusing on solutions, you can take a vital step towards leading a fulfilling and authentic life, characterised by meaningful connections and the ability to thrive in social settings.

Understanding the nature of social anxiety and its impact on individuals is crucial in developing effective strategies and approaches to manage and overcome its challenges. With compassion, support, and appropriate interventions, individuals struggling with social anxiety and agoraphobia can find relief and regain control over their lives, ultimately fostering a sense of ease and empowerment in social interactions.

The causes of social anxiety can often be traced back to the fear of negative evaluation by others, leading to feelings of embarrassment and shame. While the specific origins of social anxiety are still being explored, research suggests that negative experiences such as public shaming or failure can contribute to its development, including experiences during childhood. These key events can leave a lasting impact, causing individuals to avoid situations that might lead to potential embarrassment and to experience nervousness when contemplating social settings. The anticipatory worry further exacerbates social anxiety, and the tendency to engage in compulsive post-event rumination can reinforce and perpetuate the anxiety.

It is common for individuals with social anxiety to feel a sense of shame and reluctance to discuss their social fears. Seeking help from a therapist can be instrumental in exploring the underlying core negative beliefs that fuel social anxiety. Through therapeutic intervention, you can challenge and dispute these beliefs, learning to distinguish between assumptions and facts. For instance, someone with social anxiety might assume that others think they are weird or useless. In therapy, negative automatic thoughts can be disputed, alternative appraisals can be installed, and worst-case scenarios can be "de-catastrophised". These techniques will assist you in developing a more realistic perspective and distancing yourself from negative thoughts.

Confirmation bias also plays a significant role in social anxiety, as individuals tend to search for evidence that supports their pre-existing beliefs. With social anxiety, the focus often centres on the self, heightening bodily anxiety symptoms such as shaking, sweating, or stammering. This increased attention on negative signs perpetuates the cycle of anxiety, causing individuals to overlook positive signs of friendliness or warmth directed towards them. The inability to objectively judge social situations, and the tendency to solely focus on negative self-image, create a self-perpetuating cycle that hinders functioning in social contexts as it did for Mike's case that I shared in Chapter 10. This tunnel vision restricts individuals from fully engaging with the world around them, significantly impacting their daily lives and overall well-being.

Numerous stories like those of Bob, Lee, and Christina highlight the profound pain you may experience when faced with social situations, and the significant impact this may have on your life. Social anxiety extends beyond mere self-consciousness; if left unaddressed, it can profoundly impede you from living a fulfilling life. Recognising the origins and diagnosing social anxiety may require the expertise of a therapist, but by gaining awareness and reflecting on the content of this chapter, you can take the first step towards overcoming social anxiety and agoraphobia, seeking the necessary support.

It is important to emphasise that overcoming social anxiety is a gradual process, requiring patience, persistence, and self-kindness. Everyone's journey is unique, and it is crucial to explore and experiment with these strategies to find the ones that resonate authentically. By incorporating the *Fix Me* tools and techniques into your daily life, you can gradually overcome social anxiety, cultivate a greater sense of self-assurance, and lead a fulfilling life characterised by meaningful connections and the ability to thrive in social settings.

Fix Me Tools

Be Aware of Your Thoughts. Observe and become aware of your self-conscious thoughts in social situations. Notice when negative or self-critical thoughts arise, such as "I'm not good enough" or "Everyone is judging me." Remember that these thoughts are not facts, but rather products of your anxiety. By becoming aware of them, you can start to challenge their validity.

   Reframe Your Thoughts. Once you've identified negative thoughts, work on reframing them. Challenge the accuracy of these thoughts and replace them with more realistic and positive alternatives. For example, if you catch yourself thinking "Everyone is staring at me", reframe this by reminding yourself that people are likely focused on their own lives and not paying as much attention to you as you might think.

   Focus Externally. Shift your attention away from internal self-monitoring and redirect it towards the external environment and the people around you. Engage in active listening by genuinely focusing on what others are saying. Notice details of your surroundings, such as the decor or the sounds in the environment. This shift in focus helps to break the cycle of self-conscious thoughts.

   Expose Yourself Gradually. Overcoming social anxiety requires gradually exposing yourself to anxiety-provoking situations. Start by challenging yourself with smaller social interactions and slowly work up to more challenging situations. For example, you might begin by initiating a conversation with a familiar acquaintance before progressing to larger group settings or public speaking engagements. This step-by-step approach allows you to build confidence and resilience over time.

   Stay Mindful and Grounded. Practice grounding exercises to stay present and reduce anxiety in social situations. Focus on your breath, observe your surroundings, and engage your senses. Grounding techniques, such as feeling the texture of an object or noticing the sensation of your feet on the ground, can help anchor you in the present moment and alleviate anxious thoughts.

   Practice Positive Self-Talk. Improve a positive and compassionate inner dialogue. Challenge self-critical thoughts and replace them with kind and encouraging statements. Remind yourself of your strengths, past successes in social situations, and positive qualities. For example, instead of telling yourself "I always say the wrong things", replace this with "I have valuable insights to share, and people appreciate my perspective."

Get Social Skills Training. Seek opportunities to enhance your social skills through training programmes, workshops, or therapy. Learning effective communication techniques, active listening skills, and assertiveness can boost your confidence in social interactions. Practising these skills in a secure and supportive environment allows you to gain competence and reduce anxiety.

Build a Support System. Surround yourself with supportive friends, family, or a therapist who understands your social anxiety struggles. Please share your experiences, thoughts, and feelings with them. Their encouragement, empathy, and guidance can give you the reassurance and support you need to face social situations more confidently.

Practice Self-Care. As discussed in the previous chapter, prioritise self-care activities that promote relaxation, reduce stress, and enhance overall well-being. Participate in activities that bring you joy, such as hobbies, exercise, meditation, or spending time in nature. Taking care of your physical and emotional health allows you to approach social situations with a stronger and more positive mindset.

Designate Worry Time. Schedule time to worry—designate a specific period each day to address your worries and concerns. Choose a time that works best for you, whether in the morning, afternoon, or evening. During this scheduled worry time, allow yourself a set duration, such as 15–30 minutes, to engage with your worries actively. Sit down in a quiet and comfortable space, free from distractions, and focus your attention on your concerns. Write them down in a worry journal or notebook, allowing yourself to explore and express your worries fully. By confining your worries to this dedicated time, you create a mental boundary that prevents them from intruding on the rest of your day. It helps to remind yourself that you have set aside this time specifically for worrying, and any anxious thoughts that arise outside of this designated period can be gently acknowledged and set aside for later. This practice allows you to gain a sense of control over your worries and promotes a more balanced approach to managing anxiety.

> **Seek Professional Help.** Seek professional help from a therapist or counsellor specialising in anxiety disorders. They can provide tailored strategies, guidance, and support in overcoming social anxiety. Therapy sessions can help you explore underlying causes, create coping mechanisms, and provide a safe space to discuss and work through your social anxiety. Remember, progress takes time, so be patient and gentle with yourself throughout the journey. Celebrate even the smallest victories and continue practising.

We have explored the nature of social anxiety and its impact on individuals. We have learned that social anxiety is characterised by fear, avoidance, and heightened self-consciousness in social situations. It often stems from negative experiences, past trauma, or a fear of being negatively evaluated by others. Social anxiety and agoraphobia can be debilitating and isolating, making it challenging for individuals to navigate social interactions with ease. To overcome social anxiety, we have explored various tools and strategies to empower you and promote your well-being.

12

Bullying and Its Effects on Anxiety

In the preceding chapter, we delved into the intricacies of social anxiety and agoraphobia and its impact on our relationships. We explored the fear of judgement, self-consciousness, and the tendency to focus inward rather than on the people and situations around us. By understanding the causes and manifestations of social anxiety, we gained insights into the challenges it poses in our interactions with others.

Now, we shift our attention to another significant issue related to anxiety and relationships: bullying. While bullying is commonly associated with childhood experiences, it is crucial to recognise that it can occur at any age and in various social and virtual settings. Bullying involves intentional and repetitive acts aimed at causing harm or discomfort to another person, taking different forms such as physical aggression, verbal abuse, or more subtle manipulations that can cause extreme stress and often social anxiety.

In this chapter, we explore the harmful effects of bullying, both on the individuals who experience it and the broader social fabric. We delve into the motivations and root causes of bullying, shedding light on the underlying insecurities and power dynamics that drive it. Through this exploration, we aim to foster empathy, compassion, and awareness, creating a foundation for addressing and preventing bullying in our relationships and communities. Bullying manifests in various forms, each with its own damaging effects. Understanding the different types of bullying is essential in comprehending the behaviour of bullies themselves. Physical bullying involves direct harm and abuse to the body, conjuring images of physical violence and aggression. Verbal bullying, on the other hand, encompasses harassment, name calling, and emotional abuse, often accompanying physical bullying. It is crucial to recognise that bullying is a repetitive and targeted pattern of behaviour, distinct from mere aggression or abuse. A bully intentionally selects their victim based on specific criteria, perpetuating a cycle of torment.

By understanding the link between anxiety and bullying, we can develop strategies to promote healthier relationships, more assertive communication, and cultivate empathy and respect. Together, we can work towards creating a society that values kindness, inclusivity, and the well-being of all its members.

What Is Bullying?

Bullying is a pervasive issue affecting individuals of all ages and occurs in various contexts. It is essential to recognise that bullying is fundamentally a relationship problem, requiring relationship-based solutions involving both the bully and the victim. However, not everyone involved in bullying may be aware of their role or recognise the need for change in their behaviour. Meanwhile, the victims of bullying endure ongoing exposure to toxic behaviour, which can have long-lasting adverse effects, including increased anxiety later in life. Breaking the cycle of bullying is challenging, as it requires active sharing from all parties involved. Nevertheless, it is possible to identify the origins and dynamics of bullying through introspection and deliberate effort, and work towards its resolution.

Reflecting on my life experiences, I can recall instances of encountering bullying while growing up in the East End of London during the 1970s and 1980s. At the tender age of five, my siblings and I became targets of racial and verbal abuse from a member of the British National Party (BNP). These distressing encounters shed light on the deeply ingrained colourism and prejudice that prevailed during that time. Unfortunately, such behaviour was normalised, and I was encouraged to downplay the pain and not fully acknowledge its impact. However, as I pursued higher education, I began to develop a deeper understanding of what constituted bullying behaviour.

Although the bullying I experienced did not have a significant impact on me during my childhood, I gradually realised the psychological implications as I matured. It became apparent that the effects of such experiences can manifest differently in individuals. Many people I spoke to had become accustomed to it, finding ways to cope and not allowing it to hinder their progress or impact their lives. My siblings and I, too, accepted it as a means of coping. However, it is important to note that accepting or adapting to bullying does not make it acceptable. It was merely our way of navigating through the challenges we faced.

As I continued to explore the psychological impact of bullying, I realised that the long-lasting effects could be profound. The experiences we endure during our formative years can shape our perceptions of ourselves and others, impacting our self-esteem, confidence, and overall well-being. It is a realisation that resonates with many individuals who have endured similar forms of mistreatment.

Many individuals who have experienced this type of bullying, including me, often develop a strong inclination to please others, a psychological defence mechanism known as people-pleasing or *fawn*. The fawn response we reviewed in Chapter 7 is also linked to co-dependency. But it can also be characterised by a tendency to seek safety by appeasing and pleasing others, often at the expense of one's own needs and boundaries. This can manifest as being overly accommodating, submissive, and compliant in relationships, and avoiding conflict or assertiveness. As a result, we adapt to awkward and uncomfortable situations, believing that it is our responsibility to maintain harmony and avoid confrontation. This tendency to tolerate mistreatment can have far-reaching consequences, as illustrated by the case of Jessie.

Jessie found herself in a work environment where she consistently performed well yet was overlooked for promotions and recognition. Deep down, she sensed that she was being treated unfairly, but her ingrained inclination to please others prevented her from raising the issue. She internalised the belief that she should accept the situation, as it was a norm of the era (1970s and 1980s) she grew up in. However, through therapy, Jessie began to question and challenge this ingrained pattern. A spark of empowerment ignited within her, compelling her to take a stand against the ongoing mistreatment.

With newfound clarity and determination, Jessie decided to take legal action against her organisation. However, she soon faced the harsh reality of the legal process, realising that she lacked the financial means to sustain a lengthy legal battle. Despite this setback, her courage and resilience resulted in a small compensation. The experience served as a powerful reminder that avoiding confrontation and tolerating mistreatment can hinder personal growth and effect a cycle of injustice.

This case demonstrates how anxieties rooted in the fear of confrontation and the desire to please others can prevent individuals from asserting their rights and standing up for what is fair. It underscores the importance of recognising and challenging these deeply ingrained patterns, as they can hinder personal and professional progress.

By acknowledging and reflecting on these experiences, we can develop a greater empathy and understanding for those who have experienced bullying. It becomes apparent that supporting and advocating for those who have endured such hardships is essential in promoting healing, growth, and a society that values inclusivity and respect.

These personal encounters have forged a resolute opposition to bullies in physical and digital spaces. However, the rise of online bullies, trolls, and haters in today's digital landscape has brought new challenges. These individuals propagate negativity and engage in harmful behaviours, causing distress and anguish to their targets. Confronting and addressing this form of bullying requires intelligence, empathy, and resilience.

Fostering a culture of respect, understanding, and kindness is imperative to combat bullying effectively. We must stand up against bullies and create safe online and offline spaces. A collective responsibility requires individuals, communities, and institutions to raise awareness, promote empathy, and establish zero-tolerance policies. By working together, we can create a society that unequivocally rejects all forms of bullying, fostering an environment of acceptance, inclusivity, and mutual support.

Within the fabric of my memories, a particular incident from my childhood remains vivid. Outside our primary school, a group of older and physically imposing young adults menaced my siblings and me. We were innocent children, all under 10, and we were caught in the crosshairs of their verbal and physical aggression. During this chaotic scene, a teacher, likely my brother's class instructor, emerged as an unexpected ally, bravely intervening to protect us. Yet, these bullies, driven by their insecurities and prejudices, redirected their fury towards her, further revealing their ignorance and fear. The root of their hostility was a profoundly entrenched apprehension of the unfamiliar, expressed through unjustified animosity based solely on the colour of our skin. The teacher, on the other hand, was of the same race as them. They did not like that she stood up for three brown children. Reflecting on this episode, I contemplate how my understanding of these bullies, had it been nurtured during my early years, would have shaped my own anxieties.

Through my encounters with bullying, I have come to recognise that the mindset of a bully is often rooted in ignorance and a deficiency of emotional intelligence. It manifests limited comprehension and an inability to extend empathy and understanding to others. Bullies find themselves trapped within the confines of a narrow worldview, incapable of embracing growth or recognising the inherent value of those they target. Their actions arise from a complex interplay of insecurities and personal struggles projected onto their victims. Acknowledging one's role as a bully in a given situation is a psychologically intricate and emotionally challenging process, demanding introspection and the courage to confront one's own inner demons.

Bullying, a complex phenomenon, continues to perplex us as we seek to understand its underlying causes. As a therapist, I have extensively researched and observed patterns throughout my career, shedding light on the motives behind bullying. It is important to recognise that individuals may respond to anxiety or unfamiliar emotions in various ways, and one possible response is aggressive or defensive behaviour. Bullying can sometimes stem from individuals feeling threatened or insecure themselves, leading them to lash out or exert power over others as a way to cope with their own internal struggles. This aggressive or defensive behaviour can manifest in different forms, such as verbal, physical, or relational aggression.

However, it is crucial to note that not all individuals who experience anxiety or unfamiliar emotions resort to bullying behaviour. Many individuals may cope with anxiety by withdrawing or avoiding situations, rather than exhibiting aggression. It is also important to distinguish between temporary reactions to anxiety or stress and consistent patterns of bullying behaviour, which can have severe and lasting effects on the well-being of others.

Understanding the underlying causes of bullying behaviour, including anxiety and insecurity, can be valuable in developing interventions and prevention strategies. By addressing and supporting individuals in managing their anxiety and building healthy coping mechanisms, it is possible to reduce the likelihood of resorting to aggressive or defensive behaviour towards others.

In some cases, bullies find a perverse sense of success in their behaviour, allowing them to exert power and control over others. However, their motivations can vary significantly. Peer pressure, societal changes, or even their own history as victims of bullying may drive their actions. These factors come into play, particularly when the bully and the victim share a personal connection, as the bully intentionally selects their target. It is crucial to recognise that the responsibility for creating the bullying situation lies solely with the bully, not the victim.

In the challenging situation involving Layla, a renowned singer who experienced verbal and intentional bullying by her fellow cast members on a reality show, her agent sought my assistance to help her cope with the distressing circumstances. Without disclosing specific details, it is evident that Layla became entangled in a complex dynamic driven by jealousy and anxiety (see Chapter 9). Her people-pleasing nature played a role in her reluctance to assert herself or be dismissed, ultimately leading her to accommodate the behaviours of the instigators.

As a popular celebrity on the show, Layla's success and growing fan base may have triggered feelings of envy and insecurity among her fellow cast members. These emotions, combined with their own anxieties and potential performance-related fears, manifested in the form of emotional, verbal, and even physical bullying and abuse towards Layla. The presence of jealousy, an intense and often distressing emotion, can distort thoughts and perceptions, leading individuals to engage in harmful behaviours as they attempt to alleviate their own insecurities.

As Layla's therapist, I had the privilege of guiding her through the complex and emotionally charged situation she faced. It became evident that jealousy and anxiety were significant factors driving the bullying dynamics. Layla, with her people-pleasing nature, found herself caught up in the situation, yearning to be accepted and avoid confrontation. Through our therapeutic sessions, Layla began to develop a deeper understanding of her emotions, thoughts, and behavioural patterns.

One key practical factor that played a crucial role in Layla's coping process was the implementation of specific strategies. Together, we worked on assertiveness training, focusing on her ability to set boundaries, express her needs, and stand up for herself in the face of bullying. Through role-playing exercises and gradual exposure to challenging situations, Layla built her confidence, developed effective communication skills, and learned to navigate the dynamics of bullying with resilience and self-assurance.

Additionally, Layla benefited greatly from the support of a strong network. We encouraged her to surround herself with trusted friends, family, and professionals who provided emotional support, guidance, and encouragement throughout her journey. Their presence and understanding became a vital source of strength for Layla as she faced the complexities of the reality show environment, which she gradually moved away from.

By combining therapeutic interventions, including assertiveness training and the support of a strong network, Layla was able to regain her sense of self-worth, assert herself, and address the bullying she faced. She demonstrated remarkable growth and resilience, developing healthier coping mechanisms to navigate challenging situations. Layla's experience serves as a testament to the power of practical strategies that empower individuals to overcome adversity and reclaim their sense of agency and well-being.

Over time, our understanding of bullying has evolved. Personally, I experienced a period of respite from bullying during the 1990s and early 2000s. It seemed that both the prevalence of bullying and my own victimisation had subsided. However, as I embarked on my studies in psychology and ventured into the field of education, a disheartening realisation unfolded. Bullying had not vanished in society; it had merely transformed in the digital age. The internet brought forth new forms of aggression, most notably cyberbullying, which allowed for pervasive bullying beyond the confines of school. As a result, cyberbullying has become alarmingly prevalent and has inflicted profound trauma on its victims.

While significant attention has been dedicated to addressing bullying among children, the same level of focus is often lacking when it comes to adult bullying. During my teaching years, I witnessed countless assemblies and programmes highlighting the impact of bullying on children. In those moments, even the most notorious bullies would appear sheepish in the face of the interventions. Regrettably, many bullies fail to change their destructive patterns without genuine self-reflection and a concerted effort to address the root causes. As a result, the cycle perpetuates itself, as children who bully others grow up to become abusive adults, potentially subjecting their own children to similar torment (Johnson, 2018).

If you or someone you know has ever treated someone else so as to cause them harm, then you can relate to this next paragraph otherwise, skip this part and go on. Breaking this cycle requires you, as the bully, to embark on a challenging journey of introspection and transformation. By acknowledging the impact of your actions and undertaking genuine self-reflection to understand the underlying causes of your behaviour, you can take the necessary steps towards personal growth and change.

Cyberbullying has emerged as a prevalent form of bullying facilitated by the online realm. This insidious behaviour occurs through digital channels, allowing bullies to inflict harm and harassment from behind the screen. The dangers of cyberbullying have been widely acknowledged, as the impact of social media on both celebrities and ordinary individuals highlights the devastating consequences it can have. Victims of all forms of bullying are profoundly affected, experiencing a range of psychological distress. From depression to eating disorders, and even contemplation of suicide, the repercussions can be catastrophic. Furthermore, even without reaching these extreme outcomes, victims of bullying often develop severe anxiety disorders that persist long after the bullying has ceased. Tragically, situations involving social media bullying have even resulted in devastating outcomes, such as the case of the British TV presenter, who took her own life following online bullying. This highlights the profound and far-reaching impact of online bullying. Furthermore, the effects of bullying, whether experienced online or offline, can be equally detrimental to mental health and well-being.

The individuals targeted by bullies endure prolonged suffering, burdened by the pain inflicted upon them. Bullies deliberately select their victims, knowing they are more likely to experience pain and be less inclined to stand up against their tormentors. The profound anguish endured by victims permeates every aspect of their lives, leaving them feeling isolated, powerless, and consumed by anxiety. Remarkably, the impact of bullying can extend beyond the individual victim, affecting their entire family unit. The consequences of bullying persist long after the bully has moved on to another target, as the victim's self-esteem and sense of self-worth have been shattered.

These enduring consequences of bullying contribute to the development of anxiety disorders, further exacerbating the distress experienced by victims. The fear and trauma inflicted by bullies create anxiety, weaving its way into the fabric of their daily lives. The anxiety stemming from bullying infiltrates their thoughts, relationships, and overall well-being, leaving a lasting imprint that can be challenging to overcome.

We must address bullying comprehensively, not only in terms of the immediate harm it inflicts, but also considering the long-term implications for the mental health and overall quality of life of those affected. By fostering empathy, promoting resilience, and implementing effective anti-bullying measures, we can create a supportive and inclusive society that protects individuals from the devastating effects of bullying and alleviates the burden of anxiety.

The Impact of Bullying

The impact of bullying extends far beyond the immediate moment. Its effects linger, often leaving long-lasting scars on the victims as we saw earlier with Jessie and even myself, with our people-pleasing behaviour. One significant symptom that may emerge in adults who have experienced bullying is post-traumatic stress disorder (PTSD). PTSD occurs when the mind repeatedly brings individuals back to the traumatic event, resulting in stress, flashbacks, panic attacks, and social anxiety. Although commonly associated with traumatic or life-threatening events, such as car accidents or losing a loved one, PTSD can also stem from prolonged abuse or bullying experiences. Those who suffer from PTSD may grapple with depression, heightened stress levels, sleep disturbances, and haunting nightmares, creating a cycle of anxiety-related behaviours that persist long after the bullying has ceased.

Anxiety is a common response to bullying in children, and its chronic presence can pave the way for the development of anxiety disorders. Continuous exposure to bullying throughout childhood can have profound effects, and both educators and caregivers need to recognise the symptoms that may manifest in children. Children enduring bullying often exhibit a persistent sense of impending doom, chronic worry, and physical manifestations such as generalised anxiety disorder, insomnia, stomach aches, restlessness, fatigue, and, in severe cases, fear. The traumatic experiences suffered by victims of bullying can create a persistent anticipation of negative events, ingrained in their psyche from past experiences. The stress of constant worrying infiltrates various aspects of their lives, intensifying over time. Early recognition and support are crucial in preventing the development of anxiety disorders later in life.

It is paramount to validate the experiences and concerns of children who have been bullied. Dismissing their fears and physical symptoms can undermine their emotional well-being, teaching them to suppress their feelings and leaving them vulnerable to the onset of anxiety disorders in adulthood. By nurturing an environment where children feel heard and understood, we can foster their emotional resilience and equip them with the tools to address their challenges effectively.

Panic attacks often serve as an alarming indicator that bullying may be taking place. In my experience as an educator, back in the day, I observed that children who experienced unexpected and recurrent panic attacks often harboured intense feelings of terror, which they were hesitant to disclose. Symptoms such as palpitations, chest pain, and sweating accompanied their deep-seated fear. Over time, the frequency of panic attacks led to the development of social anxiety disorder, as discussed in Chapter 11. This disorder encompasses fear of humiliation and negative judgement from others, making it unsurprising that victims of bullying are more susceptible to its onset. The embarrassing or humiliating experiences endured during school or public functions become ingrained in their perception, leading to heightened anxiety and avoidance of social situations.

Recognising the signs and symptoms of bullying in all its forms, particularly in children, is of utmost importance. Left unaddressed, bullying can have severe consequences, including developing anxiety disorders, social phobias, and, tragically, even death. By actively listening to and supporting individuals who have experienced bullying, we can create a safe and nurturing environment that helps them heal and thrive.

Society needs to acknowledge the damaging effects of bullying and take proactive steps to prevent and address it. Educating individuals about the psychological and emotional impact of bullying, promoting empathy and kindness, and implementing effective policies and interventions are all vital in forming a culture where bullying is not tolerated. Together, we can build a world where individuals are empowered to embrace their uniqueness, treat others with respect, and foster an atmosphere of inclusivity, understanding, and support.

Fix Me Tools

For Victims—Disengage. For individuals who have experienced bullying, removing themselves from the toxic environment or relationship is crucial. This may involve assertively standing up to the bulling behaviour, as Jessie did, or disengaging from their harassment, as when Layla walked away from the reality show. In addition, coping with anxiety and its effects can be aided by engaging in creative outlets such as music, art, or writing, which serve as a means of expression and distract the mind from anxious thoughts. Finally, seeking support from a therapist or using resources like this book can also provide valuable guidance in addressing the anxiety and post-traumatic stress of bullying.

For Bullies—Know What Drives You. If you find yourself engaging in bullying behaviour, acknowledging and recognising the impact of your actions is a significant achievement. Reflecting on the underlying reasons for your behaviour is essential. What void or need are you attempting to fulfil by hurting others? Examining your own emotions, anxieties, and past experiences, and the models you have been exposed to, can shed light on the origins of your behaviour. Finally, taking the courageous step of seeking help from a therapist or professional can guide you in breaking the cycle of bullying and finding healthier ways to meet your needs.

For Adults Supporting Children—Validate. As adults responsible for supporting children, it is crucial to validate and believe their experiences. Partaking in open and honest conversations with children is paramount. Creating a safe space where they feel heard and understood allows them to express their thoughts and concerns. Seeking guidance from family members, teachers, or counsellors can provide valuable insights on the appropriate steps to support children's healing journey. It is essential to acknowledge that any symptoms or anxieties should not be ignored, as they may indicate underlying issues that require attention and intervention.

This chapter explored the often-overlooked issue of adult bullying and its lasting impact on individuals and relationships. Bullying can occur at any age and in various settings, leading to extreme stress and social anxiety. We examined the motivations behind bullying, highlighting underlying insecurities and power dynamics. The effects of bullying can be profound, resulting in anxiety disorders and post-traumatic stress. Fostering empathy, resilience, and implementing effective anti-bullying measures are crucial to address this issue. Validating victims' experiences, promoting reflection among bullies, and supporting children who have endured bullying are essential steps towards creating a kind and inclusive society. By working together, we can build a world that values the well-being of all its members, both online and offline.

Reference

Johnson, A. (2018). The long-term effects of bullying: From childhood to adulthood. *Journal of Social Psychology*, 45(2), 123–140.

13

Fear of Happiness

In this chapter we dive into the intriguing connection between happiness and anxiety. Have you ever come across the term *cherophobia*? It refers to the fear of happiness, a psychological phenomenon that involves feeling uncomfortable or intentionally avoiding positive experiences. It's fascinating to explore how anxiety can arise when encountering moments of joy, or even when anticipating feelings of pleasure. This fear of happiness can have various underlying reasons, such as the fear of disappointment, the belief that happiness is fleeting and will be followed by sadness, or a subconscious desire to protect oneself from vulnerability. Through our exploration, I aim to shed light on the intricate relationship between happiness and anxiety, allowing you to gain a deeper understanding of your own feelings towards joy and uncover strategies to navigate them.

Take a moment to reflect on your understanding of happiness, for it is a deeply personal and enigmatic concept. Have you actively explored the path of self-discovery, diving deep into the factors that influence your present state of happiness? Have you contemplated the obstacles that may hinder its enduring presence in your life? These introspective reflections serve as a guiding light as we embark on our shared exploration of the intricacies of happiness.

In the last chapter, we embarked on a profound exploration of the impact of bullying on our capacity for joy. This exploration revealed the unfortunate reality that bullies can strip away our happiness, leaving behind a lingering sense of anxiety. However, amidst the presence of anxiety, it is important to recognise that happiness remains within our reach.

Cherophobia often reveals itself as a defence mechanism, acting as a shield to protect you from potential pain or negative emotions that could accompany happiness. This fear may be influenced by past experiences of loss or trauma, leading you to associate happiness with subsequent pain or loss. Consequently, you may unconsciously undermine your own happiness, resist engaging in activities that bring you joy, or even experience guilt when positive emotions arise. It's important to recognise how cherophobia intertwines with anxiety, as it can create a cycle of avoidance and fear that hinders your ability to fully embrace and enjoy moments of happiness. By understanding the origins of your fear and working through it, you can begin to encourage a healthier relationship with happiness and alleviate the anxiety that accompanies it.

During my teenage years, I consciously chose to reject societal expectations and embraced the pursuit of authenticity as the key to true contentment. I realised that finding happiness meant staying true to myself and engaging in activities that genuinely brought me joy. One such activity was reading, which ignited a sense of excitement within me that rivalled the latest gadgets coveted by my peers. Engaging in recreational pursuits, prioritising personal growth, and seeking out new adventures became profound sources of fulfilment in my life. Even amidst personal hardships, including moments of brokenness, loss, betrayal, and trauma, I held onto the wisdom imparted by my mother, refusing to succumb to despair. One thing she said that always stayed with me, and I don't know its origins, is that when we feel buried in despair and a dark place, we are rooting ourselves, ready to grow. For me, this was profound. Instead, I actively sought out the positive aspects amidst the pain. This mindset and approach allowed me to navigate through anxiety and find resilience in the face of adversity. By focusing on authenticity and embracing activities that brought me joy, including travelling, learning about different cultures, and engaging in adrenaline-driven activities, I discovered a powerful antidote to anxiety, enabling me to cultivate a sense of purpose. I wanted to continue to grow, which eventually led me to pursue my desire to help others awaken to their drive in life.

Witnessing my mother's unwavering resilience in the face of immense challenges served as a profound lesson on the power of choice in shaping happiness. Despite enduring financial struggles and societal judgements as a single Indian woman raising four children, she found solace in the joy of having her family united and safe. This perspective, centred on gratitude and togetherness, became the foundation of her happiness, overshadowing concerns about material provisions she never had a scarcity mindset. As she instilled a deep sense of gratitude into us, we learned to embrace the beauty of each moment. To this day, she still says there are certain words we should not use, because they are the words that will define us. "I don't have enough" or "I want more than I have." She always tells us to say "I have more than enough, and I will have plenty more to come." This not only applied to money, but to life itself. To family, love, and happiness. Always encouraging each of us to be happy right now.

In the midst of our lives, where smiles, laughter, and overcoming obstacles were encouraged, we couldn't escape the awareness of underlying anxieties. The untimely loss of our father instilled a fear that happiness could be abruptly snatched away. This realisation brought both apprehension and an understanding of the value of cherishing moments of joy and finding strength amidst uncertainty. We learned to embrace the present, appreciate life's fragility, and navigate the complex fabric of emotions. Armed with this wisdom, we continued to forge ahead, treasuring every moment while confronting life's uncertainties head-on.

Having an Attitude of Gratitude

In the face of numerous challenges, my mother, a sagacious woman, exemplified resilience and strength. Despite being only thirty-two years old when widowed, with four children to care for, a hearing impairment, and minimal support from family or friends, she faced the daunting task of carrying on. People often marvelled at her ability to persevere, and when asked how she managed it all, her response was simple yet profound: "I have a choice." Reflecting on my own journey and personal development, I've questioned whether my pursuit of happiness should be tainted by fear. This introspection led me to explore various moments in my life, both positive and negative, and discover the invaluable opportunities they provided for personal growth and intense gratitude and appreciation. Embracing gratitude, even amid adversity, has profoundly impacted my overall happiness. By actively choosing gratitude and seeking change, I've realised the power to shape my own path and confidently embrace life's challenges with renewed strength and positivity. By recognising that we always have a choice, just as my mother did, we can navigate our lives with intention and embrace the possibilities before us. This is a part of what helps us manage anxiety.

From an early age, gratitude was instilled in me as a habit. My mother, despite our modest means, taught me to appreciate the simple things in life. Even when our dinner consisted of just an onion and a few chapatis (unleavened flatbreads commonly consumed in South Asian cuisine, made from wheat flour and cooked on a hot griddle or open flame), she encouraged us to treat it as a three-course meal, emphasising the power of visualisation and gratitude. This mindset of finding joy and gratitude in everything, no matter how seemingly insignificant, became essential to our survival.

Practising gratitude has deeply ingrained an immense change in my mindset, guiding me through difficult times with unwavering optimism and resourcefulness. It has allowed me to perceive invaluable lessons and growth opportunities even during painful experiences. For instance, the untimely loss of my father during my formative years granted me the precious gift of personal development, unencumbered by the weight of societal or cultural expectations. While the inherent anxiety could have overwhelmed me, my mother skilfully established healthy boundaries, allowing me to manage them effectively. With a profound sense of self-respect emanating from her, I cultivated a deep respect for her in return.

She fostered an environment of freedom for my siblings and me, nurturing our individuality within those limits. As we ventured into our teenage years, she gently reined us in only when necessary, ensuring that freedom brought us genuine joy. This significant experience instilled in me an unwavering understanding: when entrusted with the privilege of choice and lifestyle, even today, I strive earnestly to honour the boundaries set by my mother, cherishing the essence of staying true to myself.

However, there have been moments when my happiness has been questioned by others. Societal norms, cultural influences, and personal relationships can impose limitations on our ability to fully experience and express joy. Cherophobia the fear of happiness is a common struggle, stemming from the belief that happiness is fleeting and may attract misfortune. Therefore, those who are genuinely happy, as I like to believe I am, may fear it. This can be the onset of the anxiety. You see, cultural factors also play a significant role in shaping our perception of happiness and the extent to which we allow ourselves to embrace it. It's not unheard of within the Indian culture that you should not laugh too much. The elders often say this, in fear that the joy will not last and it will be "jinxed", as mentioned in Chapter 9; their fear is other people's "Nazar", or jealousy.

Acknowledging and addressing these external influences hindering our ability to embrace happiness is essential. By actively exploring and challenging these limitations, we can break free from their constraints and pursue authentic happiness. This requires self-reflection, self-consideration, and a willingness to relinquish the fear that happiness may be temporary. Embracing the idea that happiness is attainable and deserving of our full embrace allows us to live more fulfilling lives and inspire others to do the same. It is crucial to recognise and challenge these barriers to happiness. By refining gratitude and understanding that happiness is not synonymous with perfection, we can liberate ourselves from anxiety, stress, and even fear, and embrace the joy that life has to offer. Choosing to focus on the good, even amidst difficulties, can transform our perspective and enable us to live authentically.

Aiming for Progress Not Perfection

I once had the opportunity to work closely with an elderly woman named Mrs Thompson, who struggled with deep-rooted perfectionism that hindered her ability to experience true happiness. Mrs Thompson had internalised societal expectations that tied her worth to meeting impossible standards of perfection. Her fear of judgement and the need to maintain an impeccable façade prevented her from fully immersing herself in moments of joy and happiness.

Through gentle conversations and guidance, I encouraged Mrs Thompson to explore the idea of embracing imperfection and allowing herself to experience happiness without fear. This process involved examining the underlying beliefs that fuelled her pursuit of perfection and working towards shifting her mindset. Over time, Mrs Thompson began to recognise the beauty in imperfections and the importance of self-compassion. She was of a military background; her father served in the armed forces and due to his strict nature, she thought perfectionism was a means to display self-respect and discipline. As she let go of the need for perfection and opened herself up to appreciate that she had a lot to value in her life especially the experience she realised that she was happy with what was present. She started to experience a newfound sense of freedom and contentment by letting go of the restrictions she had put on herself, knowing not everything had to be perfect, especially within and around her.

It is crucial to challenge the barriers imposed by cherophobia and achieve a mindset that embraces happiness now. This can be obtained by actively practising gratitude, acknowledging the blessings in our lives, and valuing the present moment. By choosing to focus on the good, even amidst difficulties, we can shift our perspective and allow genuine happiness to flourish. Embracing imperfections, nurturing self-compassion, and challenging societal expectations are all vital steps in overcoming cherophobia and cultivating a deep and lasting sense of happiness.

As you navigate through the complexities of life, it's essential to prioritise your own happiness and well-being. Take a moment each day to savour the simple pleasures that bring you joy, whether it's sipping a cup of coffee in the morning or engaging in activities that ignite your passion, such as singing, dancing, or anything that makes your heart soar. By treating yourself with kindness and nurturing your mental, physical, and emotional health, as we explored in Chapter 10 when you delved into the concept of self-relationship, you will establish a strong foundation for lasting happiness. Embrace the power within you to create an environment that supports your well-being and radiates positivity in every present moment.

Interestingly, when we treat ourselves well and celebrate our achievements, our brains release *inhibitory neurotransmitters* that make us feel good (this was first covered in Chapter 4). When we experience happiness, several neurotransmitters are released in our brain, contributing to our positive emotional state. See the special terms below, listing the primary neurotransmitters associated with happiness.

Dopamine. This is often referred to as the "feel-good" neurotransmitter. It plays a crucial role in the brain's reward and pleasure centres. When we engage in activities that bring us joy, achieve a goal, or experience something positive, dopamine is released, reinforcing the behaviour and creating a sense of pleasure and satisfaction.

Serotonin. Serotonin is involved in regulating mood, emotions, and feelings of well-being. It helps to stabilise our mood and promotes a sense of calm and contentment. Low levels of serotonin have been connected with conditions such as depression and anxiety, while increased serotonin levels are associated with improved mood and overall happiness.

Endorphins. Endorphins are natural painkillers and mood boosters. They are released in response to stress, pain, or physical activity, such as exercise. Endorphins create a sense of euphoria, reduce anxiety and stress, and contribute to an overall sense of well-being.

Oxytocin. Oxytocin is often known as the "love hormone" or "cuddle hormone". It is released during social bonding, physical touch, and positive social interactions. Oxytocin promotes feelings of trust, connection, and emotional bonding, enhancing our sense of happiness and well-being.

Neurotransmitters and the complex interplay of psychological factors are deeply intertwined with anxiety. In the context of cherophobia, anxiety manifests as a response to the anticipation or experience of positive emotions. The fear of disappointment, the belief that happiness is fleeting, or the subconscious desire to avoid vulnerability can all contribute to anxiety surrounding happiness.

Anxiety related to cherophobia can create a vicious cycle that hinders individuals from fully embracing and experiencing joy. The fear and discomfort associated with happiness can trigger anxious thoughts, physical sensations, and avoidance behaviours. This anxiety may stem from a deep-seated belief that happiness is undeserved or will inevitably be followed by negative outcomes.

Addressing anxiety in relation to cherophobia involves exploring and challenging the underlying thought patterns and beliefs that contribute to the fear of happiness. Therapeutic approaches like cognitive-behavioural therapy (CBT) can help individuals identify and reframe negative thoughts and develop healthier perspectives on happiness. By challenging anxious thoughts, individuals can work towards overcoming their fears and embracing the possibility of happiness.

Building self-compassion and self-worth is also essential in managing anxiety related to cherophobia. Cultivating self-acceptance and recognising your inherent value can help you combat anxious thoughts and beliefs that undermine your ability to experience happiness. Practices such as gratitude and awareness can aid in shifting the focus away from anxious anticipation and towards appreciating the present moment, being there, fully engaged in the task at hand. If your mind drifts, schedule an overthinking period of time to think about the issue.

It's important to remember that anxiety is a natural response, and it can be managed and overcome. By addressing and understanding the psychological aspects of anxiety related to cherophobia, individuals can work towards creating a healthier relationship with happiness and fostering a more balanced and fulfilling life.

Fix Me Tools

Shift Your Focus. Shift your focus to the positive. Our brains have a natural inclination to notice and remember negative things, thanks to our primal instincts. However, we can train our brains to be more positive and encourage happiness. This doesn't mean ignoring reality or pretending everything is perfect. Instead, it involves choosing to notice, appreciate, and expect goodness in our lives. By consciously looking for things to be happy about and being present with positive thoughts, we can rewire our brains to focus on the good and reduce anxiety and unhappiness.

Gather Moments of Joy. Gather moments of joy, not material possessions. Change is a part of life, and while it can sometimes bring challenges, it also presents opportunities for growth and happiness. Instead of getting overwhelmed by the negatives that change may bring, focus on gathering moments of joy. Embrace the positive experiences and surround yourself with an uplifting and positive environment. This could mean spending quality time with family and friends, engaging in activities that bring you joy (like laughing yoga or dancing), or simply appreciating the little things in life. By prioritising moments of joy over material possessions, you will cultivate a sense of fulfilment and find lasting happiness.

Take Responsibility for Your Happiness. Take responsibility for your own happiness. You have the power to shape your own happiness. Take responsibility for your well-being by practising gratitude, prioritising self-care, and making choices that contribute to your overall happiness. Express appreciation for the things you have, take care of your physical health by engaging in exercise and proper sleep, and be kind to yourself. Find an exercise routine that suits your lifestyle and preferences, whether it's dancing, walking, swimming, or practising yoga. Remember, nobody is more responsible for your happiness than you are. Embrace what brings you joy and take proactive steps towards a happier life.

Share Your Happiness. Lastly, remember that happiness is contagious. When you find joy within yourself, you also have the ability to spread it to others. Express gratitude and appreciation for the kindness shown to you by others. The simple act of saying thank you can make both you and the other person feel great. Embrace the power of kindness and appreciation in your interactions with others. A smile is universal, any person of any language understands it and an act of kindness can uplift someone's day and create a positive ripple effect. So, let your happiness shine and inspire others to find their own joy.

In summary, cherophobia, the fear of happiness, can hinder our ability to fully embrace joy and happiness. By challenging this fear and feeling gratitude, embracing imperfection, and nurturing self-compassion, we can break free from the shackles of perfectionism and allow genuine happiness to flourish in our lives. It is a journey that requires self-reflection, resilience, and a willingness to challenge societal norms. By doing so, we pave the way for a more fulfilling and joyful existence as our authentic selves.

14

Calming Anxiety Through Mindfulness

You may misunderstand or dismiss mindfulness as a passing trend, but do not underestimate its power and effectiveness in managing anxiety. I know it has been mentioned often in this book, but it works. It's that simple. As a therapist, I witness first-hand the illuminating impact of mindfulness in helping individuals like yourself control the negative effects of anxiety on their lives. You see, there is no one-size-fits-all approach to mindfulness, but when you incorporate this practice in various forms, you can experience incredible benefits. So, what is mindfulness? Mindfulness is the practice of actively embracing and observing the present moment with heightened awareness (meditation), fostering acceptance, and a non-judgemental attitude towards your thoughts, feelings, and experiences.

Meditation extends beyond the stereotypical image of sitting cross-legged and chanting mantras. It encompasses various forms, such as strolling through a serene park, indulging in a good book, or merely embracing moments of silence. Meditation has been an enduring practice that has offered tremendous support throughout my life's journey. As a young child, I would witness my family convene in our cosy family room, engaging in traditional meditation as yogis often depict sitting cross-legged, eyes gently closed, intentionally creating a space of profound stillness. Although I may not have fully grasped its significance at that tender age, it was during those moments that I acquired the art of navigating my own mind. Whether the backdrop resonated with a soft melodic mantra or was enveloped in pure silence, I became attuned to my inner voice, gradually fostering a profound trust in its wisdom. This introspective harmony symbolises the harmonisation of the three brains, as explored in Chapter 4. However, I invite you to embark on a personal experience to grasp the essence of mindfulness. Allow me to share the following paragraphs: after that, you may embark on your mindfulness practice.

To experience the powerful benefits of mindfulness practice in action, find a comfortable position, close your eyes, and take a few deep breaths to relax your body and mind. Focus on your toes, intentionally tense the muscles in that area for a few seconds, and then release the tension completely. Gradually work your way up through each muscle group in your body, tensing and releasing the muscles as you go, from your feet to your legs, abdomen, chest, arms, and head. As you release the tension, feel a deep sense of relaxation spreading throughout your body. Reach a state of deep relaxation and visualise yourself in a serene setting, such as a peaceful beach or a quiet garden. Fully immerse yourself in this calming imagery, experiencing the sights, sounds, and sensations of the environment. Repeat positive affirmations or suggestions to yourself, such as "I am calm, confident, and in control" or "I release all tension and embrace inner peace." Breathe deeply and slowly, fully embracing the state of relaxation and positivity. When you are ready to end the session, slowly open your eyes, take a moment to reorient yourself, and carry the sense of calmness and inner peace with you throughout your day.

Integrating different aspects of ourselves our cognitive abilities, emotions, and intuition is vital in making informed and holistic decisions that align with our values, goals, and overall well-being.

This principle holds true across various spiritual and religious beliefs, where individuals find their own unique practices to cultivate mindfulness. For example, in Sikhism, the method of Simran involves the repetition of the word "Waheguru", meaning "Wonderful Lord" or "Wondrous Enlightener". Similarly, in Christianity, individuals may meditate on specific Bible verses. These practices aim to purify the mind, strengthen the spiritual connection, and attain inner peace and realisation.

For me, the practice of Simran has been significant. Growing up in a Sikh family, I was introduced to this practice early. I would sit in quiet contemplation, focusing on the repetitive recitation of Waheguru. Through this practice, I discovered the joy of being present and listening to my thoughts, immersing myself in Simran's peaceful and enchanting world. Simran allowed me to quiet the noise of everyday life, bringing a sense of tranquillity and deepening my connection with my inner self and being attuned to the vibrations around me. It became a personal refuge, where I could reflect, find solace, and experience a profound sense of unity with something greater than myself, what most now describe as spiritualism or a positive enlightening energy.

While the practice of Simran is rooted in Sikhism, its essence goes beyond any specific religion. It is a testament to the universal human yearning for inner peace and spiritual connection. No matter what your spiritual or philosophical beliefs may be, incorporating mindfulness techniques into your life can bring you a sense of tranquillity and allow you to connect with your inner self and the world around you.

As I grew older, I encountered challenges and moments of pain that naturally elicited fear and anxiety. However, my early exposure to meditative practices provided me with effective coping strategies. It wasn't until later, when mindfulness began gaining popularity in the Western world, that I realised I had been practising it all along without labelling it as such. Being present and letting go of worries about the future were ingrained in me from childhood. Yet, as adulthood brought forth new responsibilities and anxieties, the teachings of my past served as a reminder to release unnecessary concerns. Mindfulness became a tool to redirect my attention to the present moment, a space of safety and calm that could help manage and even replace anxiety.

It is worth noting that some may argue mindfulness is overrated or outdated. However, this viewpoint fails to recognise the profound impact mindfulness can have, particularly in managing anxiety. By reflecting on the previous chapter about the fear of happiness, we can appreciate how mindfulness complements the pursuit of happiness by refining a deep connection with the present moment. Mindfulness is not just a passing trend; it is a powerful tool that can guide us towards inner peace and transform our relationship with anxiety.

By incorporating mindfulness into your life, you can develop a greater sense of self-awareness, find solace in the present moment, and effectively navigate the challenges of anxiety. Let us now explore the depths of mindfulness and uncover its potential to empower and uplift you on your journey.

Mindfulness is a transformative practice that allows you to shift your focus from the worries of the future or the regrets of the past and anchor yourself in the present moment. It provides a refuge from the incessant chatter of your mind and offers a way to better understand and manage your emotions. By cultivating awareness of your physical and mental state, mindfulness empowers you to respond more skilfully to challenging situations, making it particularly beneficial for those struggling with anxiety.

But why does mindfulness work? Although the concept of simply being present may seem straightforward, true mindfulness requires dedicated practice and effort. However, the rewards are profound. Mindfulness invites you to embrace and accept your emotions without judgement, enabling you to identify and process them more effectively. By becoming fully present in your body, you can let go of anxious thoughts about the past or future, allowing these concerns to dissolve away.

There are numerous ways to engage in mindfulness practice, with the common thread being the intentional focus of attention on the present moment. For some, like me, meditation serves as a foundational practice. However, mindfulness can also be a part of your daily activities. Take cooking, for example. Engaging mindfully in this task involves immersing yourself completely in the process noticing the aromas, flavours, and techniques with full attention. The key lies in controlling and directing your attention, which is the essence of mindfulness.

Mindfulness will not only transform your relationship with the present moment, but also shape your perception of self. In Buddhist psychology, the concept of self is viewed as fluid and ever evolving. It recognises that our thoughts and mental events are malleable, a notion supported by the concept of *neuroplasticity* the brain's ability to change. By engaging in mindfulness, you can reframe negative beliefs and behaviours, rewiring your mind towards more positive patterns. Remarkably, research conducted at Harvard has demonstrated that mindfulness practices can actually alter the wiring of the brain, aiding in the recovery of individuals suffering from depression. This highlights the profound impact mindfulness can have on your mental well-being, empowering you to nurture and optimise your brain's functioning.

Practising mindfulness is powerful as a means to manage anxiety and promote overall well-being. It extends beyond being a mere buzzword or religious concept, offering practical tools for cultivating happiness and mitigating the negative effects of anxiety. For me, mindfulness practice has increased my self-esteem, confidence, and self-acceptance.

I wanted to dedicate the majority of this chapter to the range of mindfulness practices—including breath awareness, body scan meditation, mindful walking, mindful eating, journalling, and mindful listening—elucidating how these techniques ground us in the present moment, enhance awareness, and foster a deeper connection with ourselves and the world. It is vital to remember the importance of consistency and seeking professional guidance if you need more support.

Fix Me Tools

Be Aware of Your Breathing. Awareness is a fundamental aspect of mindfulness. The breath serves as an anchor, grounding us in the present moment. By directing our attention to the sensation of the breath as it enters and exits our body, we develop a heightened sense of awareness and connection to the present. This simple yet profound practice can be done anywhere, anytime, making it easily accessible for incorporating mindfulness into our daily lives.

Be Aware of Your Body. This practice involves systematically directing our attention to different parts of the body, bringing a gentle and non-judgemental awareness to each area. By scanning the body from head to toe, we cultivate a deep sense of bodily awareness, fostering a greater connection between mind and body. This practice can help us release tension, observe bodily sensations without attachment, and give a sense of gratitude for the incredible vessel that carries us through life.

Walk Mindfully. Walking is a practice that involves bringing mindfulness into our physical movements. Whether we are walking in nature or simply going from one place to another, we can build awareness of each step, the sensation of our feet touching the ground, and the subtle movements of our body. By engaging in mindful walking, we are invited to fully submerge ourselves in the present moment, observing the sights, sounds, and sensations around us.

Eat Mindfully. Eating is another practice that can bring greater awareness and appreciation to our relationship with food. Rather than eating on autopilot or rushing through meals, we can practise mindfulness by savouring each bite, observing the colours, textures, and flavours of the food, and being fully present with the act of nourishing our bodies. Mindful eating allows us to develop a deeper connection with our food and our body's signals of hunger and fullness, leading to a more balanced and mindful approach to eating. If food is chewed mindfully, this also helps with our gut health, making our digestive intelligence more receivable.

Keep a Journal. By putting pen to paper, we create a space for self-reflection and introspection. Through the practice of mindful journalling, we can explore our thoughts, emotions, and experiences with curiosity and a lack of judgement. This process allows us to gain insight into our patterns of thinking and gives us a greater sense of self-awareness. I can relate to this, as writing this book has made me learn so much more about myself.

Practice Mindful Listening. Mindful listening is a great practice that can deepen our connections with others and enhance our overall mindfulness experience. In our technology-driven and fast-paced world, we often find ourselves engaged in conversations without truly listening or being fully present. Mindful listening involves giving our complete attention to the person speaking, without interrupting or formulating responses in our minds. Instead, we aim to be fully present, open, and receptive to what the other person is expressing. To practise mindful listening, we can start by focusing on the sounds and tones of the speaker's voice, noticing the subtle nuances and inflections. We also pay attention to their body language and non-verbal cues, gaining a deeper understanding of their emotions and intentions. By letting go of our preconceived notions, judgements, and distractions, we create a safe and supportive space for the speaker to be heard and understood.

Mindful listening not only fosters more meaningful connections and empathy, but also allows us to gain new perspectives and insights. Through this practice, we can develop a better gratefulness for the richness and diversity of human experiences. By being fully present in our interactions, we can nurture healthier relationships and foster a sense of compassion and understanding in our communication with others.

Incorporating mindful listening into our daily lives needs conscious effort and a readiness to let go of distractions. It may be helpful to set aside dedicated time for deep listening, whether it's during conversations with loved ones, colleagues, or even listening to podcasts or audio books. By approaching listening with a sense of curiosity and openness, we can hear about more mindful and enriching experience that enhances our overall well-being. Remember, mindfulness is a versatile practice that can be applied to several aspects of our lives. Exploring different techniques and finding what resonates with you personally is key to establishing a sustainable mindfulness practice that supports your well-being and personal growth.

In addition to the *Fix Me* tools, mindfulness can be infused into daily activities such as washing dishes, brushing teeth, or even engaging in creative pursuits. The key is to approach these activities with a sense of presence and attentiveness, fully immersing yourself in the present moment and observing the sensory details of each experience. While these tools and practices can serve as valuable foundations for mindfulness, it is important to remember that mindfulness is a journey of self-discovery and exploration. Each individual may resonate with different practices and techniques, and it is important to find what works best for you. Regular practice, consistency, and patience are essential in reaping the benefits of mindfulness. Over time, mindfulness becomes more than just a practice it becomes a way of being, permeating every aspect of our lives and fostering a deep sense of peace, clarity, and connection with ourselves and the world around us.

15

Calming Anxiety Naturally

We've reached the end of our journey together. Congratulations! You've taken a step towards healing yourself and growing into the best version of who you are. As you approach the final chapter, take a moment to pause and reflect on the profound pilgrimage you have taken thus far. But before we delve into the depths of this concluding chapter, in the previous chapter we learned that the concept of mindfulness is truly enlightening. It can calm your mind remarkably and draw you closer to a state of inner serenity.

Now, direct your attention to this chapter, where we will revisit the essential lessons you have learnt, guiding you towards the realm of natural remedies that provide solace in times of unease. Within these pages, you will venture into the realm of calm, exploring holistic approaches that beautifully harmonise. So, let us continue this captivating sojourn together, embracing the wisdom that unfurls and discovering a life filled with tranquillity, fulfilment, and boundless possibilities.

Instead of resisting or fighting against anxiety, consider why you hold onto it (maybe a deep-rooted fear of change or the unknown). Anxiety can become a familiar companion, even if it hinders your progress, because you find comfort in its familiarity. Maybe as a way to seek attention or validation from others, unknowingly creating a self-fulfilling prophecy where your belief in anxiety perpetuates its presence. Although releasing anxiety may seem challenging, it is the key to experiencing freedom and happiness. Embrace the possibility of letting go and transforming your relationship with anxiety.

Let me introduce you to Sally-Anne, one of my clients, who found herself in a similar predicament. She was once married to a renowned celebrity, but suspicions of infidelity consumed her thoughts, and she clung tightly to these fears, afraid to let go. Imagine yourself tightly grasping a handful of sand, desperately trying to hold onto every grain.

Even after their divorce, Sally-Anne continued to hold onto the fear of abandonment, unwilling to release her grip on the past. Just like trying to hold onto the sand, her anxiety slipped through her fingers, leaving her empty and exhausted. It became clear to her that holding onto anxiety was futile it only caused frustration, hindered her growth, and prevented her from experiencing the freedom and peace she longed for.

Years later, when her ex-spouse announced a public marriage, Sally-Anne realised she needed help. Her anxiety escalated again, leading to more frequent panic attacks. In therapy, we discovered that she was resistant to letting go because her fear served a purpose for her. It provided her with a sense of safety and the attention she craved. The timing of seeking therapy coincided with her ex-spouse moving on, which triggered even more anxiety. However, she soon learned a valuable lesson: her intention to hold onto the fear of loss ultimately cost her a healthy and fulfilling relationship. It was a poignant realisation because she believed her anxiety kept her safe and protected.

In the present moment, Sally-Anne is actively working on releasing her grip on anxiety, understanding that it no longer serves her well. Through therapy, she is learning to let go of the fears that have held her back and embracing the opportunity to cultivate a healthier mindset. Acknowledging that holding onto anxiety is and by letting go counterproductive, she opens herself up to new possibilities and has a greater sense of inner peace.

Now, I pose a simple question to you: Are you willing to let go? The prospect of hearing a resounding "YES" in response fills us both with excitement and anticipation. The essence of this book was to empower you, just as I have learned to empower myself. As we draw near the culmination of our journey, where anxiety and self-discovery intertwine, I wholeheartedly express my deepest gratitude for allowing me to accompany you along this transformative path. With utmost admiration, I bear witness to your remarkable growth and unwavering resilience. I implore you to embrace the profound wisdom that resides within you adopt it fully, empower yourself, and emerge as the incredible individual you are destined to be.

Embracing anxiety involves acknowledging its presence in your life and accepting it as a part of your experience. It's about facing anxiety with courage and compassion, rather than avoiding or suppressing it.

Empowering yourself in the face of anxiety seeking ways to manage and overcome it involves having healthy boundaries in place and building resilience. It's essential to develop coping strategies, changing and letting go of anything that doesn't serve a purpose for you.

Emerging signifies the transition process of letting go of your old self and familiar patterns and adopting new habits. The process of transformation is challenging, but the process of rising above anxiety is phenomenal. It represents the idea of coming out stronger, wiser, and more adaptable on the other side. Through the strength you have built on this journey, the self-growth you have gained, you can emerge from anxiety's grasp and finally tame that villain within and release the superhero you are.

Throughout our shared journey, you have delved into the depths of self-awareness and introspection, unravelling the intricate threads that bind you to anxiety. With each step forward, you have honed your ability to recognise and understand the triggers that once held sway over your emotions. This newfound self-awareness has given you the power to choose your response, freeing yourself from anxiety's grip.

In your pursuit of healing, you have unearthed the remarkable potential within you. With unwavering determination, you have managed anxiety and taking back the control you need in your life, guided by the knowledge and insights gained along the way. Accept this power, for it is your birthright to take control of your mental well-being and enjoy a life of serenity and fulfilment.

Remember to accept the present moment fully as you continue on your journey. Let go of regrets from the past and worries about the future, for it is in the here and now that true transformation occurs. You can channel your energy into creating your desired life by grounding yourself in the present.

Self-acceptance stands as a beacon of liberation on your path to healing. Embrace every facet of your being, honouring your strengths and weaknesses alike. Embody the beauty of imperfection, for it is through acceptance that true growth and change can flourish. You are a unique and extraordinary individual deserving of love, compassion, and understanding. Hold onto your authenticity and let it shine brightly in all you do.

As you navigate the complexities of your existence, remember to practice self-compassion. Be gentle with yourself as you encounter setbacks and challenges along the way. Treat yourself with the same kindness and understanding you would extend to a dear friend. By nurturing a compassionate relationship with yourself, you create a solid foundation for healing and growth.

In this moment, as we bid farewell, I encourage you to carry the wisdom you have gained into every aspect of your life. Adopt your loved ones and foster deep connections with those who uplift and support you. Celebrate the gift of each precious day, living in a perpetual state of gratitude for the abundance surrounding you.

Within you lies the power to change your life and fix yourself by understanding yourself better. Your past does not define you, and your anxieties do not limit you. Embrace the truth that you have the ability to shape your reality, creating a life brimming with purpose, joy, and profound fulfilment. Embarking on each moment as an opportunity to live boldly, love fiercely, and fully welcome life's extraordinary journey. Though we part ways, remember that you are never alone. Seek support from loved ones, therapists, or support groups when needed. Surround yourself with a community that nurtures your growth, releasing the pain, revealing your true self, and renewing your life.

Release anxiety, as you have learnt that it only arises when you hold onto negative thoughts, worries, and fears. Releasing refers to letting go of these burdens and allowing them to dissipate and lose their grip on your mind. By releasing anxious thoughts and emotions, you create space for something new and positive to enter.

Once you let go, you create an opportunity to uncover deeper truths about yourself and your situation. The act of revealing involves self-reflection, introspection, and gaining clarity. It is through this process that you can gain insights into the root causes of anxiety and understand your triggers, discovering healthier ways to manage it.

Renewal follows this and signifies the transformative aspect of overcoming anxiety. It implies a sense of growth, rejuvenation, and positive change. By releasing anxiety and revealing your inner strength and resilience, you open yourself up to renewal and the possibility of a more peaceful and happier life now. Renewal also involves adopting coping mechanisms, practising self-care, and using kind words to yourself. Such self-talk is positive, reassuring almost like an older and wiser version of yourself. Some refer to this as the "higher self".

In the depths of anxiety, you embarked on a inspiring journey of self-discovery, reclaiming your power and seeking solace from within. Along the way, you explored the intricacies of your mind, delving into the triggers and patterns that held you captive. With each step, you embraced self-awareness, self-acceptance, and self-compassion, unleashing the transformative potential that lay dormant within you. Through various strategies and tools, you empowered yourself to manage anxiety and take control of your life, gently guiding yourself towards healing and growth. You learned to let go of the fear that kept you trapped, embracing the unknown with an open heart and mind. By rewriting your narrative, setting intentions, and cultivating resilience, you harnessed the strength to face anxiety and emerge victorious. You recognised that self-discovery is ongoing, with ups and downs, setbacks and triumphs, but you embraced the beauty of this duality and your unique story, knowing that you hold the pen to shape your destiny. As we bid farewell, we celebrate the profound transformation that has taken root within you, as you step forward into a future brimming with possibility, love, and completion.

Remember, you have the power to manage anxiety and take control of your life by incorporating these tools and strategies into your life. Enjoy the journey of self-discovery and growth and know that you are not alone in this process. With determination, self-compassion, and the right support, you can overcome anxiety and live a more fulfilling and joyful life.

Many individuals hold onto their anxiety for various reasons, and it can be challenging to let go without the right knowledge and tools to address the underlying feelings. Some may not know how to deal with overwhelming emotions, while others may lack awareness of their own triggers and coping mechanisms. Seeking therapy or medical assistance is essential for some, while others explore alternative therapies and treatments. Whatever you choose, remember to follow your gut feelings, as this will guide you to make the right choices for yourself.

Each person's experience with anxiety is unique, shaped by their personality, environment, and cultural background. It is crucial not to compare your situation with others, as everyone's journey is different. However, one common factor among all individuals is the storage of emotions and memories in our minds. Often, anxiety becomes intertwined with emotions such as shame, grief, sadness, embarrassment, or anger. These emotions get suppressed or pushed into the unconscious mind, making it challenging to address the anxiety itself.

Sally-Anne's case exemplifies how anxiety can be deeply rooted in past experiences and memories. She held onto her anxiety surrounding her ex-spouse, refusing to let go of the fear of divorce. It became a safety net for her, providing attention and a sense of protection, even though it hindered her ability to move on. Unconscious memories can resurface when triggered by certain events even something as small as a smell or a song. These triggers ignite fear and anxiety, leading to a fight, flight, freeze or fawn response.

Understanding the connection between our mind and body is crucial in addressing anxiety. It's essential to be kind, positive, and loving to ourselves, focusing on gratitude and appreciating the present moment. Alongside the changes discussed in this book, implementing lifestyle changes can further support anxiety management and promote overall well-being.

When addressing anxiety and seeking sustainable solutions, it is essential to consider the role of diet and nutrition. It is common for individuals to resort to substances or specific foods as a temporary means to alleviate anxiety or numb their underlying emotions. However, these coping mechanisms are not effective in the long run. For instance, caffeine acts as a stimulant that can trigger anxiety symptoms, while substances like alcohol and nicotine merely offer temporary relief without addressing the root cause. Instead, exploring natural remedies such as Bach Flower Remedies or herbal teas can provide support without the risk of developing addictive tendencies. The significance of our dietary choices should not be overlooked, as certain foods can contribute to stress levels and worsen anxiety symptoms. Remember, what you put into your body influences your digestive intelligence, affecting your mental well-being. A healthy gut-brain connection leads to a healthy head brain and heart brain, as explored in Chapter 4. Therefore, maintaining a balanced diet, staying hydrated, and being mindful of our eating habits can positively impact our overall cognitive intelligence and give a feeling of vibrance and clarity.

It's important to acknowledge that anxiety cannot be fully treated by simply altering our mind's perception of memories. Prescription medications may be helpful in some cases, but they only address the symptoms rather than the underlying emotions. To truly overcome anxiety, it's necessary to delve into those emotions, bring them to the surface, and address them directly.

In addition to lifestyle changes, there are interesting strategies that can help manage anxiety. For instance, during panic attacks, manipulating your environment can provide a sense of calm. Gravity or weighted blankets have been found to have a calming effect on individuals with anxiety. These blankets use deep-touch pressure stimulation, which stimulates pressure points in the body, promoting relaxation, mood improvement, and better sleep. It is important to research and choose responsibly when considering using gravity or weighted blankets, as individual experiences may vary.

Finally, addressing anxiety involves a comprehensive approach that encompasses self-reflection, therapy, and lifestyle changes. By being aware of how we use substances, addressing our eating habits, and exploring unique strategies like gravity or weighted blankets, we can take steps towards managing anxiety and achieving a more balanced and joyful life.

Incorporating supplements and vitamins into your daily routine may offer additional support in managing anxiety. However, it is important to consult with a healthcare professional to ensure their suitability for your specific needs and any potential interactions with existing medications.

Remember, embracing the journey of self-discovery involves exploring a variety of strategies and approaches to find what works best for you. By combining self-reflection, self-compassion, seeking support, mindfulness, setting healthy boundaries, practising self-care, adopting a growth mindset, and exploring alternative remedies, you can embark on a path towards understanding, resilience, and inner peace.

Afterword: Embrace the Power Within

As we come to the end of this meaningful journey, I want to express my deep gratitude for being a part of your path to self-realisation. Together, we have explored the complex maze of anxiety, uncovering your incredible potential. As our paths separate, I encourage you to embrace self-awareness, self-acceptance, and self-compassion, empowering yourself to find inner peace.

Throughout our journey, you have become more self-aware, understanding the roots of the anxieties you feel and gaining insight into your own mind. With this wisdom, you have the power to navigate life's challenges, purposefully shaping your life's story. You now step into the role where you can manage anxiety and take control of your life, discovering the courage to face your fears, nurture your bravery, and maintain unwavering confidence amidst the ups and downs of life. You should now know who you are, continue learning what you desire, and appreciate what you fulfil.

Before we part ways, take a moment to reflect on the trigger test (Table 1.1 in Chapter 1) that started this change. Let its lessons guide you in your continued self-discovery and personal growth. By recognising the triggers that once had a hold over you, you can celebrate your progress and appreciate the positive changes that have taken root within you.

In the grand story of life, accepting yourself as you are is the key to liberation. Acknowledge your imperfections, honour your vulnerabilities, and celebrate every aspect of your being. This profound self-acceptance will give you the courage to embark on an authentic and fulfilling journey. As you navigate life's complexities, cherish the growth that comes from being kind to yourself. Embracing your unique path will lead to genuine healing and limitless personal growth.

As we conclude this transformative journey, I want to express my heartfelt appreciation for allowing me to be a part of your experience. May the wisdom shared here serve as a guiding light, illuminating your path and strengthening your belief in your own resilience and untapped potential.

With every step you take, embrace the gentle wisdom of self-compassion, cherishing your existence. Embrace setbacks as opportunities for growth and fulfilment. Remember, you have the power to write your own narrative, capable of rewriting your story with each passing moment.

Fix Me is an invitation to realise that the power to heal and transform resides within you. Hold your loved ones, celebrate the gift of each day, and live with gratitude for the blessings surrounding you. Embody the profound truth that you can create a purposeful, joyful, and deeply connected life.

Know that your journey continues to unfold, offering endless possibilities. May each day become a testament to your strength. Lastly, cherish the beauty of your unique story, remembering that you are the author of your own narrative and that every moment presents an opportunity to live boldly, love deeply, and celebrate an extraordinary life.

"Belynder Walia is a dedicated Psychotherapist, Author and Speaker on a mission to develop inner harmony through the power of self-relationship and emotional empowerment. Her insightful guidance sparks transformative growth, promoting resilience and well-being."

Index